The Power of the Playwright's Vision

Blueprints for the Working Writer

The Power of the Playwright's Vision

Blueprints for the Working Writer

GORDON FARRELL

HEINEMANN
Portsmouth, NH

Heinemann
A division of Reed Elsevier Inc.
361 Hanover Street
Portsmouth, NH 03801-3912
www.heinemann.com

Offices and agents throughout the world

Library of Congress Cataloging-in-Publication Data
Farrell, Gordon.
    The power of the playwright's vision : blueprints for the
    working writer / by Gordon Farrell.
      p. cm.
    ISBN 0-325-00242-8 (pbk.: alk. paper)
    1. Playwriting. 2. Drama—Technique. I. Title.
    PN1661.F37 2001
    808.2—dc21

                                                2001024213

Editor: Lisa A. Barnett
Production editor: Sonja S. Chapman
Cover design: Cathy Hawkes, Cat & Mouse Design
Manufacturing: Steve Bernier

Printed in the United States of America on acid-free paper
05 04 03 02 01 VP 1 2 3 4 5

Kathleen Farrell Meyer

Who introduced me to the arts
Whose unhesitating support makes all things possible
My mother

Contents

Contents

Acknowledgments

The Yale School of Drama

The academic foundation for the ideas and structures presented here was laid down at the Yale School of Drama. Of greatest importance to the development of this book were the lectures and seminars of Professor Leon Katz. In his tenure at Yale, Professor Katz shaped a generation of dramaturgs and playwrights. When you hear Yale-trained scholars speaking clearly and concisely about dramatic form, with constant reference to structure and interdisciplinary influences, you know they were at YSD during the Katz years.

New York University

The Department of Dramatic Writing of the Tisch School of the Arts at NYU provided the principal support for my growth as a scholar. The enthusiasm and nurturance of my department under the successive chairs of Janet Neipris and Mark Dickerman made it possible for me to develop and flesh out the ideas in this book, exposing them every step of the way to the passionate young writers of DDW's student body. My first eight years there, under Professor Neipris, were particularly indispensable to the development of this book.

Marymount Manhattan College

MMC's Division of Fine and Performing Arts completed the trinity of supporting institutions that made this book possible. In particular, the Theatre Department under the chair of Mary Fleischer gave me the opportunity to include my ideas in the curricula for developing actors and directors, the emerging young practitioners of theatre production. Their enthusiasm, support, and feedback provided the final test of these ideas. In theatre arts, Aristotle was right about one thing at least: truth is a shared phenomenon. What is good for playwrights will be good for actors and directors as well.

1

The Playwright's Vision

Every work of art is an attempt to make contact with at least one other human being. Whether completely abstract or richly realistic in its details, art is one man or woman saying, "I have experienced something, I have witnessed something, I have survived something—and I need to know if it's as important to you as it is to me."

On a deeper level, the artist is also saying, "I have recognized certain things to be true about life—and I need to know that I'm not alone in feeling this way."

The artist sits down to create—writes a play or a poem, paints a canvas—because this experience, this perception about life, is too complex and too personal to be expressed in any other way. Tennessee Williams, for example, might have simply said, "When parents cling too tightly to their children, they only succeed in damaging them or driving them away," and left it at that. But this simple statement, as true as it is, does not capture the complexity of his personal experience and his personal recognition about the underlying truth of parent-child relationships. In fact, when we reduce his great play *The Glass Menagerie* to such a simple statement, we risk trivializing his insight and making it easy to forget.

Instead, Williams took his personal anguish—the characters in the play are based on himself, his mother, and his sister—and forged it into a timeless work of art that is neither trivial nor easy to forget. Imagine what his feelings must have been when he saw it performed on Broadway to international acclaim. He had touched not one other person, but millions of people, who, with their thunderous applause, said, "Yes, you're right. I have felt it, too."

Even abstract art is driven by the same basic urge of the artist to make contact with others and to share his or her perceptions about life.

The great expressionist painter Wassily Kandinsky, one of the pioneers of abstract art, tells us at length in his writing how his recognition of certain truths drove him to search for a universal, symbolic language with which he could communicate those truths in the most powerful way possible.

Kandinsky saw our life on earth as a journey through storm and devastation to a higher land, toward a safe, sacred, and eternal place. Borrowing images from the story of Noah's flood, he worked for years to develop a set of brush strokes that, even though they cannot consciously be recognized as a great boat, a tempestuous sea, and a landscape of soaring mountains, nevertheless produce in the viewer the same feelings those images would evoke if seen rendered literally in the stained-glass window of a cathedral.

He found a way to make certain his audiences felt what he felt, and shared in his vision of the world. Whether you agree with him or not is beside the point. You cannot stand in the presence of his painting *Composition VIII* and not feel stirred, ascendant, and at peace.

Over the years, working first as a painter, then as a director in the theatre, and finally as a playwright and screenwriter, I have known many artists who would deny this simple assertion that we create to communicate with others. They would insist that they create only for themselves. Poets and painters, I think, have been the most likely to take this position. It would be rash of me to try to speak for all of them. However, I believe that in the great majority of cases, this is a posture they have assumed to protect themselves from rejection. Since they need to create, whether anyone "gets" their art or not, it's important for them to shield themselves from the trauma of not being understood. We cannot all be lucky enough to be received like Tennessee Williams.

Poets and painters are fortunate in this. They can legitimately assert that they create only for themselves and it's pretty hard to contradict them.

People who work in the theatre, however, can't protect themselves in this way. Actors, directors, and designers all know that unless their work can attract and hold an audience, they have failed. In fact, our word *theatre* comes from the Greek *theatron*, which is the place where the audience sits.

Very simply, without an audience, it isn't theatre.

This is why playwrights must write for audiences. If your work fails to get produced, or being produced fails to touch an audience, then you have failed, at least in some degree, as a playwright.

Playwrights must write in a way that speaks to, and makes contact with, other people. That's the tremendous challenge faced by dramatists today.

Fortunately, we at the start of the twenty-first century are coming on the heels of one of the most innovative periods of playwriting the world has ever known. For the last two hundred years, extraordinary and inspired dramatists have been smashing the old rules, embracing new styles, and pushing the envelope of what you and I can do onstage. Because of the innovation, experimentation, and ingenuity of the playwrights who came before us, we have at our disposal some of the most powerful tools ever created for enabling us to reach our audiences.

Good thing, because never before have audiences been so hard to reach.

Dazzled on every side by movies, computers, television, and other entertainment media, audiences are increasingly reluctant to be drawn into theatres. Yet some playwrights have been able to attract them. Hit plays continue to be written every year by writers such as August Wilson, Tony Kushner, Brian Friel, David Mamet, Paula Vogel, Wendy Wasserstein, and Nicky Silver, to name a few. So it's only appropriate that we ask ourselves: what are they doing right?

The answer is twofold.

First and foremost, these are all playwrights who have a powerful vision of the world that they are not afraid to put onstage. Secondly, they have the technique to actually accomplish this.

More than at any other time in history, today's playwright must have a powerful, personal vision to drive and give shape to his or her art. I believe the reason for this is that we, as a society, lack a unifying vision of life, which we would all share in common. So there is no given sense of order in the world, no defaut assumptions about life and truth that the playwright can fall back on to give his or her work a powerful, meaningful shape. Without a powerful, meaningful shape, any work of art becomes messy and confusing.

It lacks immediacy.

It lacks impact.

In earlier periods of history, this was often less of a problem. The majority of people in any society tended to agree on one, orderly system that explained the universe. Consequently, in the past, it was often easier to write a play than it is today. And it was easier for a play to find its audience. The playwright had an inherent, unconsciously learned vision of the world that was transmitted to him or her as a child, and it usually matched the audience's vision. From this link, this agreement between the playwright and the audience about the true nature of life, the play derived its power.

This is why it is so difficult, for example, for audiences today to understand Greek tragedy—because the vision of life reflected in those plays is not one we subscribe to today. In Athens, in the fifth century B.C., people believed without question that a single human being could take action that would change his or her life and even bring harmony to the universe as a whole. Greek tragedy writers tried to show the audience the inverse as well: through action, they argued, we can also destroy our lives and undermine the harmony of the universe. Either way, the Greeks believed that our actions affect not only our own lives but the order of the cosmos itself. That's how important they felt individual human beings are in the grand scheme of the universe. By the twentieth century, we no longer felt this way about the significance of individual human behavior, and that change in our perception of ourselves contributes to the difficulty we have in understanding or enjoying Greek tragedy.

In Shakespeare's time, the English people perceived their world as being made up of multilayered strata that operated independently of one another yet somehow, through Providence, produced harmony in the nation of England as a whole. Shakespeare's history plays are con-structed to reflect this vision. Through multiple story lines, we follow characters who live in completely different social classes, speaking in radically different ways, holding radi-cally different values, and often feeling no particular warmth or affection for the people in the higher or lower social class, yet somehow producing a mosaic nation that rises to over-come every threat posed to it.

These types of differences apply when we look at the plays from other cultures, as well. Japanese Noh theatre, for example, reflects a model of reality based on Buddhist teachings. Among other things, it seeks to put us through the experience of losing our individual identities and achieving a sense of oneness with the universe. The Hindu Sanskrit theatre of India, on the other hand, assists us in preparing for reincarnation according to very esoteric rules of Hinduism. These are plays based on visions of the world to which few Westerners educated in an industrialized scientific culture would subscribe. But, to the audiences for which they were written, they are just as real and seem just as reliable as the visions that guide us through life here in the West.

When a play has a powerful effect on an audience, you can be certain it was shaped and informed by a powerful vision of life.

And when the playwright's native culture does not provide such a unifying vision of life—when his or her culture is as fragmented and as individualistic as ours is—then the playwright must use his or her own personal vision to give the work unity, shape, and power.

This is the state of affairs you and I have inherited here in America. But this situation did not occur overnight. It is the culmination of shocking, traumatic events that have shaken all of our earlier belief systems, events that began with the Industrial Revolution and continued through the two World Wars, the Great Depression, the Holocaust, the explosion of the A-bomb in Japan, and the rise of the Cold War.

Throughout this time, playwrights like Henrik Ibsen, August Strindberg, George Bernard Shaw, Lady Augusta Gregory, Samuel Beckett, Lillian Hellman, Bertolt Brecht, Jean Paul Sartre, Ed Bullins, Amiri Baraka, and Harold Pinter all developed powerful new writing tools that empowered them to capture their personal visions of the world onstage. They learned how to infuse their plays with that unifying vision of life that society had not provided for them. And they developed specific writing techniques for accomplishing that elusive but all-important goal.

The purpose of this book is to help the working playwright understand what those techniques are and to make them available to empower today's playwrights in capturing their own personal visions on the stage.

You, as an artist, have experienced things—you have witnessed things, you have survived things—that drive you to create. You have come to recognize that certain things are true about life. Like all artists, you need to know if what you have experienced and learned is as important to the rest of the world as it is to you. This is what we mean when we say a playwright has a vision. Vision is nothing more than a powerful feeling about the world and humanity's relationship to it, a feeling forged through the experiences and insights of the individual artist.

A common mistake that playwrights make is to try to express their visions—their experiences and insights—exclusively through the use of dialogue spoken by characters onstage. Philosophical conclusions or wise observations about life are one of the most tedious things an audience can be subjected to. The young or emerging playwright quickly discovers that, in fact, there is no better strategy for driving audiences away. No doubt this is because if there's one thing we learned during the twentieth century, it is *not* to trust someone else's ideas about how we should live our lives. From the rantings of Hitler and Mussolini to the great propaganda machine of Communist Russia to the scientific manipulation of consumer habits by Madison Avenue, we've all been burned by following other people's notions about truth. Out of necessity, I think, we have developed what might be called a knee-jerk skepticism about any ideas that are obviously being foisted on us by others, especially strangers.

So how *do* you capture truth in a play in a way that will be powerful and effective to audiences? After all, you're not a dictator or a multinational corporation selling dubious consumer goods; you have valuable, hard-learned conclusions about life you need to share with others. You have a vision.

The most successful playwrights have always known that they must not try to persuade their audiences with words alone. You have to show them what you have learned about life, onstage, right before their eyes.

That means you must construct your play so that all of the elements in it function in the same way you have come to believe the world itself functions.

Playwrights for the last two hundred years have been learning important new ways of doing this. The most powerful and timeless theatre we know was written by those men and women, and the lesson we learn from studying their plays is as simple and as extraordinarily difficult as this:

> Place onstage the events, the characters, and the words the characters speak in such a manner that they affect one another in the same way you, the playwright, have come to realize the world itself operates.

This is *showing*, not telling.

With this book, you will become familiar not only with the different visions those great playwrights have brought to the stage but also with the writing techniques that enabled them to do it.

Every play is a reflection of how the world works.

When you sit down to write a play, you must make certain it reflects the way that *you* have come to believe the world works. You must make certain it reflects your vision.

2

The Vision Understood

What is your vision of the world? To ask this is to ask, How do you believe the world operates? What rules do you believe govern the events that occur in our lives? Even if you say, "I don't believe that *any* rules govern the way the world operates; it's all completely random," remember that randomness itself operates by certain rules. Some things are simply more likely to happen than others. If we didn't believe this, we wouldn't have the courage to try to cross a busy street. We'd never get into elevators or cars. We wouldn't be able to plan a single event.

Furthermore, if you said to me, "I don't believe that any rules govern the world," I would point out that, in fact, you believe in gravity. If you drop something, it will fall. And I would quickly go on to add other rules of physics that you would undoubtedly accept as basic to the world's governance.

Most of us, however, do not need to start out with these basics. For most of us, discovering or articulating exactly what dynamics we believe drive the events that occur around us involves subtler and more complex questions. For example:

> Can a human being ever really produce change in this world? If so, how? Through logical, step-by-step activity or through sudden, spontaneous inspiration? By ruthless, self-interested action or by always trying to be fair and do the right thing?

If the answer to that first question is no, and you do not believe that human beings can cause change, then you must ask:

> Does change *ever* occur? If it does, what causes it? Divine intervention? Or does change occur simply by chance?

And this is only the tip of the iceberg. Forging a working sense of your personal vision is very likely to involve a process of recognizing that certain answers to the above questions apply in some cases but not in others. For example, you may believe that you can cause changes in your health by taking certain medicines—that antibiotics, if taken in the proper manner, will cure an infection. But you may not believe that working hard at your job will result in getting ahead in life. These are two very different notions about our capacity to produce change in the world, and yet they might simultaneously be held by the same person.

Where do these different visions of life come from?

That is, of course, an extremely difficult question to answer, and any answers we do arrive at will vary a great deal from one person to the next. Yet there are certain constants or reasonable assumptions we can start with. For example, the very first sense we develop about the rules that govern the world are to a large extent transmitted to us by our parents, our guardians, or the governing circumstances of our early childhood. The first rules we learn about how the world works are quite simple. They include the following:

- Caretaker adults, such as mothers and fathers, are supposed to nurture and protect us.
- Meals are served at certain times.
- Streets are dangerous.
- Unacceptable behavior gets punished.

Needless to say, as we get older, our experiences modify those simple notions, and we come to recognize that more complicated dynamics govern the world. We learn that certain kinds of behavior, under certain circumstances, will elicit desirable or undesirable responses. We learn that certain rules govern success in school. We learn that even more complex rules govern the process of job hunting.

But these are all surface manifestations of a deeper sort of rule learning that is going on at the same time. That deeper set of rules is shaped by the way in which our experiences are filtered through our emotions, then organized and interpreted according to our personal philosophical dispositions.

I say *organized and interpreted,* but I do not mean that this is a conscious activity, nor do I mean any rigorous or formal sort of *philosophy* when I use that word. What I mean, rather, is that our individual personalities give us each a unique outlook on life, and that outlook shades and colors the lessons we draw from every experience we have. Two people sharing a traumatic experience like a crime or a natural disaster, even if they are side by side all the way through it, might very easily learn different things from it—and each will come away with his or her vision of life altered in a different way.

In addition to this, the way people around us react to an event will affect how we react, and that in turn will alter the lesson we learn from it. One family's way of dealing with the death of a loved one, say, might differ greatly from another family's, but each way of coping with death will alter or reinforce the assumptions about life held by every member of that family.

In other words, our experiences, the experiences of those around us, and the unspoken assumptions of the society we live in all work together to shape, deep inside us, a model of how reality works—a vision of life.

Generally speaking, this vision will tend to be unique and personal. But does that mean there are no shared truths to which we all subscribe? Not at all. There are many ways in which our feelings about life will overlap those held by other people, especially with people raised in the same culture.

One significant truth we can point to, which is shared by people raised and educated in our culture, is our tendency to believe in physical causality. A simple example of believing in physical causality is the assumption that if we're careful drivers and maintain our automobiles properly, we will avoid traffic accidents. This assumes a strict relationship between physical activity and physical consequences.

But that is a belief system peculiar to the type of industrialized scientific culture that has proliferated in the last two or three hundred years, particularly in Europe and America. Let's say, instead, that we lived in medieval Europe. In that case, we would believe that accidents are caused by God, and the way to avoid them is to always be in a state of grace. We would not see accidents as being an extension of *causality*, but as an extension of *morality*.

Another example:

We believe that a proper diet and lots of exercise will lead to a longer, healthier life. Again, this is physical activity that leads to physical consequences. In medieval Europe, however, long life and good health were gifts from God. They were a reason to honor and glorify Him, not to pat ourselves on the back for our healthy lifestyles.

This causal view of the world that we have can extend to social causalities as well. We tend to believe, for instance, that sending our children to good schools will secure them good jobs and that correct social behavior will elicit the high regard of those around us and so lead to opportunities and social relationships we might not have had otherwise.

But this is only one vision of life. In the industrialized West, and specifically in America, there are many others. Although many people do believe in physical causality—and feel, for instance, that through causality we can change the world to make it a better place—others believe that the true causes of things in this world can never be known and that events are never really influenced by our actions. Still others believe that no meaningful change of any sort ever occurs. The more things change, the more they stay the same.

Each of these different visions has been expressed by playwrights in the theatre using different playwriting styles. Realism, naturalism, expressionism, and absurdism, among others, are major playwriting forms that were developed to show onstage significantly different ideas about the nature of life and the dynamics that govern reality.

Each was developed to place on the stage a radically different vision of life.

To make matters more complicated, many playwrights have blended and intermingled these dramatic forms. A realist play can have absurdist touches. A naturalist play can use realist techniques. Expressionism and surrealism can be intermingled with melodrama. But these techniques for expressing the writer's vision of life are what give shape, power, and authority to the writer's work.

In the following chapters, we will examine the most important models of how reality works that we have brought with us into the new millennium, focusing on how they affect the art and the craft of playwriting. By understanding these models, the playwright will be empowered to select the dramatic form that suits his or her own feelings about the world. The playwright will also see how he or she can modify, intermingle, or blend those forms together in order to find a unique voice.

Generations of Americans raised on television dramas and situation comedies are often ill-prepared to make sense of theatre. In the theatre, we re-create dramatic worlds that are radically different from the narrow version of reality shown on TV. Television tends to be dominated by a commercialized form of realism. In the theatre, however, whole other visions of reality hold sway. The commercialized realism of television tends to be shaped by the tangible and the knowable, but in the theatre there are vast and magical landscapes—the realms of our psyches, our dreams, our emotions, and even our religious hopes.

The purpose of this book is to express those visions as separate and distinct playwriting blueprints and so give the playwright the necessary techniques for putting his or her own personal vision of life on the stage.

3

Realism

R ealism is the playwriting form in which we express the belief that problems in this world can be understood and solved.

This is an approach to playwriting created by men and women who believe it is possible for you and I to produce change in the world by taking action. As I mentioned before, not everyone believes this, and many of those who do believe it feel it's true only under very specific circumstances. You may believe, for example, that going on a diet will cause you to lose weight. But you may not believe that voting will change a single thing in our political system. Yet, there may be actions that you do believe would cause political change. If so, how do you express that onstage?

Successful playwrights who yearn to promote change in the world, more likely than not, will turn to realism or some modified form of realism. Their particular vision of life tells them that change is possible, and so they use the most powerful dramatic form available to them to communicate that to an audience.

Realism was specifically created to empower playwrights to examine a problem and to promote a solution to that problem.

Note the phrasing here: *to promote a solution to that problem.*

The realist play does not *tell* us the solution to a problem. The realist play does not offer solutions of any kind. The purpose of a realist play is to show us the *causes* of the problem, period. By doing this, the realist play empowers the audience to go out and find its own solution. This is an extremely important point to remember. Even if you believe you know the solution to the problem your play is examining, you must refrain from telling us what it is. Audiences do not want to be preached to. Instead, you must motivate them to seek the solution for themselves.

If you have a message you want to communicate in your play, remember this: The message is embodied in the structure of the play, not in the speeches delivered by the characters. You communicate your message by making certain that every element in your play interacts with every other element in a way that *dramatizes* your vision of life. In this way, you show us instead of just telling us.

This is a distinctive characteristic of modern art in general, that is, avoiding the temptation to tell the audience the solution to the question the artist has raised. You must avoid the assumption that there is one universal truth that can be disseminated to an audience. No, each member of the audience must find his or her own truth, his or her own solution to the problem. The African American poet-playwright Ntozake Shange touches on this in her most influential play, *For Colored Girls Who Have Considered Suicide When the Rainbow Is Enuf.* In this play, she brilliantly dissects the problems of growing into adulthood as a woman of color in the late twentieth century. But Shange refrains from telling her audience how to solve those problems. Instead she says, in the last line of the play, that women of color are "moving to the ends of their own rainbows."

In other words, you don't have to consider suicide. You have your own truth, and you will find it yourself.

Though not strictly written in the realist manner, *For Colored Girls Who Have Considered Suicide When the Rainbow Is Enuf* is a great modern play. Like all modern art—including novels, poetry, painting, and sculpture—it refuses to give us the answers to the questions it has raised. Although in realism the drama unfolds in a world in which it is possible to know the causes of our problems, the audience still must be left to identify its own solution.

And to promote change in the world—whether it's sweeping political change or modest, personal change—first you must persuade the audience that it lives in a world in which change is possible.

When realism first appeared in the 1850s, its original purpose was to help solve problems like poverty, prostitution, failed marriages, and crime, by dissecting those problems onstage. Consequently, these types of plays are often referred to as social problem plays. Since the nineteenth century, the applications of realism have expanded to include psychological problems, class and gender problems, as well as problems of race and personal identity.

The realist play is particularly well-suited to promoting the idea that our problems can be solved. But this is true only when the playwright, by using realist technique, shows us onstage a world in which it is actually *possible* for problems to be solved. That is to say, a world in which:

1. The causes of our problems can be identified.

2. We can be confident that our actions will cause things to happen.

As I mentioned earlier, not everyone believes in number 2. In some circumstances, yes, we believe our actions will cause things to happen, for example, if I push a lamp off a table or if I snatch a child out of the path of an oncoming automobile. But in many situations we simply don't believe our actions will cause any significant change. So the realist play must show us a world in which *x* will cause *y* to happen as surely as pushing a lamp off the table will cause it to break, or as significantly as snatching a child from traffic will save a life.

Many of the most powerful and well-respected plays of the last two hundred years are written in the realist style. The greatest playwright of the last two centuries, Henrik Ibsen, made his mark on the theatre by initially writing in a strictly realist manner. His masterpieces are immortal works of drama, especially his "social problem plays," like *A Doll's House, An Enemy of the People, Ghosts,* and *Hedda Gabler.* These plays are exquisite models of realist playwriting that examine the failure of democracy, the consequences of subordinating our personal needs to society's rules, and the forces in our society that lead to the destruction of gifted women. His powerful use of the realist style inspired playwrights throughout the world. George Bernard Shaw and Lillian Hellman are among those who, following Ibsen's example, wrote timeless drama in the realist manner.

It's interesting to note, however, that after a long string of successful plays, Ibsen set out to write a realist drama in which he would actually reveal the answer to the problem he'd be examining. In his seldom-produced *Lady from the Sea,* the protagonists tell us that they have solved the problem of failed marriages—and the effect, artistically, is nearly disastrous. This particular play is redeemed by other, brilliant aspects of Ibsen's writing, but when the characters tell us the "secret of having a successful relationship," it is a tremendous disappointment for the audience and an extraordinarily awkward moment on stage. The play simply loses its credibility at this point.

Remember: Realism equips the audience to go out and find a solution. It never offers a solution itself.

Not all attempts to deviate from a strict realist model have failed. Many playwrights have successfully added to it and modified it with their own visionary insights. An example of this can be found in the work of Tennessee Williams. Williams shows us a world in which it is possible to know the causes of our problems, but it is impossible to solve them. The ultimate goal of plays like *A Streetcar Named Desire* and *The Glass Menagerie* is to confront us with the recognition that sometimes problems can't be solved because they're too deeply rooted in human nature. In this way, he broke from the traditional realist model. However, by using a realist form, Williams made that final moment of realization far more powerful than it would have been otherwise.

Another great realist playwright, Arthur Miller, also made an indelible mark with dramas such as *Death of a Salesman*, *All My Sons*, and *The Price*. As with all realists, the power of Miller's writing stems from the belief that it is possible to produce change in the world through the words we speak and the deeds we do. In his plays, Miller challenges his audience to examine and reject the idea that, as Americans, we must place economic prosperity and social respectability above everything else. He shows how misguided this assumption is and how, by following it, we create misery for those we love the most.

Although realism asserts that it is possible to change the world through our actions, it is not the only type of theatre that is based on this perception. Melodrama, a highly charged variant of epic structure, is one of the most important dramatic models of the last two centuries and the basis of virtually all Hollywood screenwriting. Like realism, it is based on the belief that people can produce change in the world. But it follows rules different from those in realism, as it demonstrates the way in which change is produced. Classical drama is another playwriting model that shows how change can be caused by people, but, again, it is different from realism or melodrama. Its focus is on our relationship with fate and the gods. One type of classical drama, tragedy, asserts we can produce change, but we will inevitably make things worse by doing so.

All dramatic forms that are based on the belief that meaningful change is possible—realism, epic drama, and classical drama among them—employ what we call an *action structure.*

Action structure, to a dramatist, simply means a structure that builds to a significant change, step by logical step. Realist drama has its own specific variation of action structure. In realist drama, the type of action structure used shows us *scientifically verifiable* cause and effect. Everything that happens to the characters—every event that alters their lives—is caused by something that flows in a logical, objectively verifiable way out of the preceding words or actions of the characters.

In realism, the world is a place in which x causes y to happen.

And, if x causes y, then y can be prevented.

How?

By changing x.

It is a tremendously powerful argument to make. Realism accomplishes it by presenting, in the structure of the play itself, a cause-to-effect universe in which every part is essential and every part contributes to the ultimate outcome, like a superb Swiss timepiece in which all the gears run beautifully and nothing is extraneous. Every hammer and every lever is necessary, and every component contributes to the final climax. The result is a type of play that is almost austere in the world it presents onstage. Four or five characters. One or two settings. Action compressed into a minimum amount of time, often showing events that come to a head and resolve themselves in a matter of days, or even hours, after the first scene.

The playwright who has a realist vision of the world sees a world of closely interconnected causes and consequences. He or she works to strip away all the nonessential elements of the story so that those causes and consequences are revealed as sharply as possible.

Summary of the Realist Vision

In the following outline, you will find summarized the key characteristics of realism as a form that expresses our belief that it is possible to produce change in the world through action. I have used an outline to keep the text distilled and convenient, like a handbook or a technical manual. Consequently, other than the major realist works cited previously, I have left out examples. What follows here (as in the other chapters) is intended to be used like a recipe. The mark of good cooks is that they will alter the ingredients to produce their own distinctive creation.

Realist Action Structure

Realism is one of several playwriting styles that uses an action structure—a structure in which the deeds or words of the characters cause things around them to change. Listed here are the features of the action structure that are distinctive to realism.

1. Every scene, without exception, builds to a moment when something changes.

- The change might be emotional: someone has an uncontrollable explosion of anger or tears.
- The change might be physical: someone is physically harmed or sees the symptoms of a disease on his or her body.
- It could be a perceptual change—a moment when one character realizes something he or she didn't know was true: a character reveals he was lying about *x*, or a revelation from the past is brought to light.
- It could be an intellectual change: a character is persuaded to believe something new.

2. These changes are never caused by random events, chance, or persons outside the story. These changes are caused only by one of two things:

   - what the characters in the play have said or done to one another
   - the underlying condition on which the play is premised.

3. The changes that occur in the first scenes trigger larger, more significant changes in the subsequent scenes.

4. These larger changes trigger the biggest change of all—a single, climactic change that alters, to some degree or another, every character in the play.

5. After the largest change—the climax—we get a glimpse of what life will now be like for the characters and the world they inhabit.

The realist action structure provides the fundamental underpinning of the realist vision. But additional features must be included in order to exploit fully the realist model. The following features are the qualities that truly get to the heart of realism. By following these rules, playwrights like Ibsen, Miller, Strindberg, and Shaw have created unforgettable visions of a world where human beings truly shape the world they live in, for better or for worse. It is a vision particular to the realist model. Recent writers who have shared in this vision include Wendy Wasserstein and August Wilson.

6. All extraneous elements are stripped away from the story. Only characters, scenes, and events that are necessary to the plot are left in.

   • There are no characters who just deliver the mail, stop in to say hi, or pass by on the street.

   • There are no scenes intended only to provide comic relief or set a mood.

   • There are no events or occurrences in the characters' lives shown in the play except those that have a direct bearing on the plot.

7. Every character is fully developed, with a complex emotional and intellectual life. There are no walk-ons and no servants, unless the servants are fully developed and integral to the plot.

8. Every character has a story with a beginning, a significant moment of change, and a wrap-up.

9. Every element of the play is resolved before the final curtain.

- All the characters' stories are brought to a conclusion.
- All of the major images are tied up.
- All of the thematic questions are clarified.
- Nothing is left dangling.

10. The major antagonists of the play—those characters who have been blocking or trying to defeat each other's attempt to produce change—must have a scene in which they confront each other face-to-face.

Background to the Development of Realism

The first realist playwrights appeared in 1850. They set out to put into practice the principles espoused by a new science, sociology, invented by the French philosopher Auguste Comte. Basically, Comte believed that the purpose of science was to improve life for human beings and that in order to do this, all of the sciences had to work toward understanding the dynamics of human society. He believed that human interaction in a community is governed by fixed and knowable laws. With the proper research and commitment from all the sciences working together, these laws could be identified and understood.

In this way, the causes of poverty could be understood. The causes of crime could be understood. The causes of child abuse could be understood, and so on. Once the causes are understood, the problem can be solved.

Thus, Comte was embracing a belief in progress that characterized almost all nineteenth-century thought and scientific activity.

Progress, purely and simply, is the notion that paradise on Earth will occur only when human beings use their

God-given intelligence to create it. It is the ultimate fruit of the scientific revolution, which began in the seventeenth century when Western scientific method was created by men like Sir Isaac Newton and René Descartes. For example, when Isaac Newton published his great work, *The Mathematical Principles of Scientific Philosophy*, he described precisely, with elegant mathematical formulas, the laws of gravity.

No one had ever done this before.

No one had ever predicted the movement of the planets as well as the movement of solid bodies on Earth, with such unerring accuracy—and the effect on the Western scientific imagination cannot be overstated.

Because of Newton's work, we in the West acquired a new model of reality. We came to see the universe as a vast, intricate, but ultimately *knowable* machine. We came to believe that everything in the universe is caused by something that can be identified, labeled, and measured.

It is as though we thought the cosmos worked like a vast clockwork mechanism.

If something in the clockwork doesn't operate properly, we can locate the malfunctioning gear or the stuck lever and fix it.

From this time forward, Western thinkers became obsessed with ferreting out all the laws that govern nature's operation. Many of the modern sciences that today we take for granted did not exist prior to this new movement. Biology, zoology, and geography were all attempts to label, classify, organize, and therefore understand the natural world in a scientific manner. Darwin's theory of evolution is an attempt to understand the diversity of life through a clockwork mechanism of heredity and environment. Sigmund Freud sought to label and categorize the components of the human psyche in the same scientific manner. When Auguste Comte invented sociology, it was part of a long line of new sciences that sought to expose the inner workings of things in this world, for the betterment of the human race.

Playwrights were particularly excited by Comte's theories, and they saw an opportunity to take part in this process of making society a better place. They began to write plays that lay bare the causes of our social problems. Prostitution, drunkenness, poverty, and crime were among their favorite topics. The idea was to raise the audience's awareness of the causes of these problems, but not to offer any solutions themselves. Rather, the audience was to leave the theatre believing it now had the knowledge to solve the problem and so set about doing it.

Theatre was not the only art form affected by the new interest in realism. To some extent, nearly all of the arts were changed by this fascination with showing a scientific version of reality to the public. In areas as diverse as painting and opera, realism called for an approach to art that was not acceptable before 1850. It demanded that its artists and its audiences take a close and objective look at life.

Even if a subject matter is squalid and repulsive, it must still be presented with unflinching accuracy. If a subject matter is beautiful and uplifting, it can be shown to be so, but no subject matter should ever be artificially forced to appear pleasing merely out of deference to the audience's sensibilities.

Realism also requires that its plays be set in a time period that is contemporary to the writer. How else can he or she claim to be accurately presenting the real world? And, for the same reason, it must be set in ordinary locales.

Realism would eventually be attacked by other modernist styles, like expressionism, absurdism, and naturalism. But no other modern style is as effective at identifying and attacking social ills, articulating the need for justice and equality, and advocating change. Consequently, realism and modified forms of realism have become extremely popular styles for the theatres of minorities and marginalized groups in our society. African American playwrights, for example, have since the 1950s used realism or realist-inspired forms to identify for audiences the causes of racism and economic oppression, thus using theatre as a way of helping solve the problems faced by the black community in America. Similar movements have occurred in Hispanic theatre, Asian American theatre, and Native American theatre. The theatres of gay men and lesbians use a realist-inspired voice to help solve the problems faced by their groups, as does women's theatre. Often playwrights in these groups will blend other styles in with the realism. Sometimes the mandate to advocate change will be the only realist component that survives in the newly mutated dramatic form, but the legacy of realism, and the belief that we can solve our problems by raising the consciousness of our audiences, continues to thrive and inspire serious dramatists in every corner of our society.

4

The Epic

T he epic vision of life, as expressed onstage, shows us a world of multiple story lines. These stories unfold in various locations at widely disparate times, often with different sets of characters. All of the characters we meet are pursuing independent goals that somehow intersect, in often unpredictable ways, to alter one another's lives dramatically. The epic world is a sprawling place in which strict cause-to-effect actions play a role as they do in realism, but coincidence, accident, and poetic justice can be just as important. And in this way it is a very different place from the world envisioned by the realists. Where the realist strips away all of the unessential parts of the play in order to reveal the underlying cause-to-effect nature of the problems afflicting its characters, the epic dramatist believes that life is too complex for those kinds of simple diagnoses to be made in a reliable or predictable manner. The realist might show us three people in a room, operating independently of the rest of the world as they shape and influence one another's lives. To the epic dramatist, that vision of life simply seems false.

Epic structure is related to realism in at least one way, however: both visions accept that change is real and that it is caused by the knowable acts of human beings.

The realist believes that once we've identified the cause of a problem, we can predict it. This, in turn, gives us the power to avoid it.

But in epic drama, although we can know with hindsight what caused events to occur, we could never have predicted ahead of time what they would be. Why? Because the world is too complex.

How does the epic dramatist capture this vision onstage?

To portray this kind of dense complexity, it is usually necessary to have two, three, or even four story lines unfolding independently of one another. It is usually necessary to show events transpiring over a length of time—weeks, years, or perhaps even decades. And it is necessary to visit many different locales in order to follow those myriad events.

That is the essence of an epic play.

Dramatists who have used this form effectively in recent years include David Henry Hwang, Tony Kushner, Peter Shaffer, and Wendy Wasserstein. Tony Kushner, for example, uses epic construction to tell the tale of two very different, unconnected people struggling with AIDS. In his *Angels in America, Part One*, we follow Prior Walter and Roy Cohn—characters who don't even know each other—through personal journeys of fear, denial, acceptance, and grief. Along the way, we meet two other men coming to terms with their homosexuality, as well as the women in their lives, who must come to terms with it also. In this complex vision of an interrelated world, there is a great sense of how each of us unwittingly affects the unknown people who are connected to the people we do know.

This, in and of itself, is a powerful metaphor for the spread of AIDS.

In other words, Kushner wanted to dramatize how we can unintentionally wreak havoc on people we don't even know through the transmission of disease, and he does this not by preaching or lecturing, but by showing us a world in which all relationships operate by the exact same rules that govern the spreading of a virus.

That is what makes *Angels* such a powerfully constructed play.

And epic structure is the only structure that could have delivered the goods in so natural and unforced a manner. At no time do we feel we are witnessing unacceptable coincidences, although there are many in the play, and at no time do we feel we're watching unconnected stories, though most of them are. Why? Because these things are natural to the epic vision of life and to epic structure.

Wendy Wasserstein, in *The Heidi Chronicles*, exploits different features of this form in order to show how a young woman in the late twentieth century navigates her way through life as she develops a personal philosophy and a sense of identity strong enough to allow her to find her own path to happiness. There are three major relationships for Heidi in this play: that with Peter, that with Scoop, and the collective relationship she has with her women friends. Her career could even be considered her fourth major relationship.

Early in the play, Heidi makes decisions to become entangled romantically with Peter and Scoop, as well as to maintain a proactive involvement with the circle of female friends she has acquired over the years. These are decisions the consequences of which Heidi cannot know in advance, and yet much heartbreak and disappointment could have been avoided—especially in the cases of Peter and Scoop—had she made different choices.

In the true epic vision, however, we cannot predict these things ahead of time.

Nevertheless, all of these relationships, involving nineteen characters, spanning a period of twenty-four years, occurring in locations spread across Chicago, New England, and New York, serve to gradually enlighten Heidi about some aspect of her own needs. This sprawling outer structure, for playwright Wasserstein, parallels Heidi's inner personal journey. In other words, the epic structure allows the protagonist's internal journey of personal growth, to be literally reflected in a physical journey through time and space.

Once again, the playwright's vision—the playwright's message—is communicated to us by making certain that the elements of her play interact with one another in the same way she herself believes the world works.

In the epic vision of life, change—or at least the potential for change—is a very real presence. Change can be extreme and sensational. In *Angels in America*, we learn in the first scene (following the rabbi's opening monologue), that foul-mouthed, down-and-dirty Roy Cohn wants to use his influence to get meek-and-mild Joe Pitt a powerful job in Washington. Big change. In the first scene in which we meet Louis and Prior, we learn that Prior has AIDS and is in a rapidly worsening condition. Big change. In the very next scene, we learn that Joe's wife is an unstable psychotic and that Louis is planning to abandon Prior.

These are sensational moments. And Kushner's play is full of them; almost every scene has a shocking event of this sort in it. Some of them are actual changes that occur in front of us, and some of them are revelations of things that have already happened, but they function exactly like changes because we're just learning about them for the first time.

These sorts of stunning plot twists are often a feature of the epic form. They are part of the legacy of nineteenth-century melodrama. Unfortunately, in the nineteenth century, so many plays using this device were so badly written that the term *melodrama* has come to have negative connotations. What prevents *Angels in America* from seeming like bad melodrama is the playwright's skillful use of other writing techniques, which are intermingled with the epic form. Surrealist and expressionist touches, for example, are used to add layers of sophistication. But these sorts of extreme plot twists are not the only type of change that can be reflected in epic plays.

The Heidi Chronicles, by contrast, is remarkable for its use of subtle and often undetected changes, changes we are sometimes not even aware of until a subsequent scene has already begun or is nearly finished. When Heidi meets Scoop, for example, we're convinced she has no intention of going to bed with him, until the last instant of the scene, when she changes her mind without even a word of dialogue. Later on, we learn that though Scoop is getting married, he still yearns for Heidi, but it doesn't cause him to break off his engagement. We learn about Scoop cheating on his wife in a similarly muted way.

Whether it is subtle or sensational, change is central to the epic vision of life.

But there is one distinctive characteristic that typifies the kind of change—or the potential for change—we find in the epic style of writing, and it's this: In the epic form, the story will typically pivot on events that the protagonist could not anticipate or exercise direct influence over. The protagonist's life is shaped for better or worse by events the character did not influence but *could have* if only he or she had known about them. And this will be the case even though some of the changes in the story are indeed brought about and controlled by the protagonist.

Later on, we will examine what I call a vision of futility. In that section of the book, we'll look at stories constructed almost completely around events over which the characters have no control. In the plays of Anton

Chekov, for example, the characters' lives are shaped primarily by the environment and social milieu of late nineteenth-century Russia. As in an epic, this is certainly a factor over which they have no control. Also as in an epic, there are multiple story lines that unfold over a period of many years. But we do not think of Chekov's plays as being epic, nor are they ever called epic. There are a number of reasons for this, among them the fact that a key epic quality is missing from his plays: even if the characters know that the social and economic environment is what's destroying them, there's nothing they can do to change it. In the epic style, by contrast, the things that trip us up—or that bring us unexpected aid—are indeed things we could have exercised control over if we had only known about them sooner.

The epic, then, can be a marvelously suspenseful form of writing. Shakespeare knew this better than anyone. In *Romeo and Juliet*, the plot hinges on a letter that goes astray, a letter warning Romeo that Juliet's death had been faked by Friar Lawrence. Here is a great example of what I'm talking about, because unlike the environment of Chekov's Russia, there's nothing inherently uncontrollable in getting that letter delivered properly to Romeo. In a gripping production of *Romeo and Juliet*, in fact, we in the audience will often feel the urge to get up onstage, take the letter from the forgetful Friar John, and deliver it ourselves.

In the epic vision of life, the world is a frustrating and difficult place because it is simply too complex to exercise any real control over the events that shape our lives.

One of the most successful dramas written with epic vision in this century is Robert Bolt's *A Man for All Seasons*. In this play, Thomas More is appointed chancellor of England by King Henry VIII. But the king is planning on divorcing the queen, a move that More deeply objects to. More hopes to satisfy both his monarch and his conscience by not speaking out on the subject at all. But he is a man with such a high moral reputation that his silence is deafening. The king insists that More must publicly approve of the divorce or be put to death, but he can't have such a well-known man executed for simply disagreeing with him. He must find a legal pretext.

More manages to avoid the legal snares set for him by the king's agents until, by a series of coincidences, one of those agents, Thomas Cromwell, gets possession of an expensive goblet that had been given to More as a bribe. This gives the king the excuse he needs to carry out More's trial and execution.

As you can see, everything pivots on that goblet reappearing and being used as evidence against More.

In fact, More had not accepted it as a bribe. He had disposed of it in an appropriate manner. But Cromwell is able to twist the facts sufficiently to have More put to death.

Thomas More was a brilliant scholar and statesman, and if he had known how that goblet was going to be used against him, he could have prevented it from happening. Unfortunately, we simply can't anticipate everything. Life is too complicated. And that is the vision of the world captured in the epic form. More is unable to anticipate or control this life-altering event because it occurs through the separate actions of another character in a subplot.

Because we are shown that the world is a place in which events—even controllable events—cannot be anticipated, we never get the feeling from an epic that we can produce change; we never say to ourselves, "Oh, if only I do *this* in my own life, then *that* can be avoided." We never feel that if we occupied a public office and wanted to avoid ever being tainted by accusations of improper conduct, watching *A Man for All Seasons* would teach us what to do. Instead, we are struck by More's relative helplessness to escape his enemies once they have set out to get him.

Remarkably enough, however, we are not depressed by this recognition.

Nor are we depressed by Prior Walter's and Joe Pitt's inability to control the events in their lives. Nor do we feel depressed by Mozart's persecution at the hands of Salieri in Peter Shaffer's *Amadeus* or by the futility of the crushed insurrection in *Les Misérables*, to use two other recent epic-style scripts as examples.

Why is that? After all, what could be more depressing than to learn you have no control over the things that are going to destroy you?

The truth is that the epic form has the potential to be incredibly uplifting and exhilarating, even when its protagonists are defeated, and this is for a very good reason: in the epic vision, people are rewarded or defeated on the basis of an overarching moral framework that ultimately determines whether the "uncontrollable" events that shape our lives have a good effect or a negative effect on us.

In the epic vision, *causality* is replaced by *morality*.

No better example of this can be found than in *A Man for All Seasons*. In the character of Thomas More, Robert Bolt has created a multidimensional persona whose motivations and psychology operate on several different levels. Among other things, Bolt is examining the character's relationship to his religious beliefs and the extent to which More actually trusts God to do—or not to do—the right thing. Because More doubts whether God will truly watch out for him, he has placed his final trust in the laws of England. In the playwright's design of the play, this is the very thing that trips the character up in his quest to resist endorsing King Henry's divorce. The law states clearly that as long as More remains silent, the king must assume that he gives assent to the divorce whether or not he really does. More, however, fails to anticipate the way in which Cromwell will subvert the law and so send him to his death.

The greater issue in the play, then, is the question of More's wavering religious faith—his inability to trust that God would see him through this troubled time, turning instead to the law for protection he ought to have sought in his maker. Couldn't we say *that* was the cause of More's failure, and if only he'd put his faith in God he could have prevailed? Isn't that the one thing More could in fact have changed and so secured a happy ending for himself?

Certainly, Robert Bolt has created a play in which we are meant to ask ourselves this very question. And it was dazzlingly provocative of him to do so; remember, Thomas More is a saint, an icon of the Roman Catholic religion, and an actual historical figure honored for centuries because of his deep religious beliefs. Yet, here comes Robert Bolt, telling us that More died because he *lacked* religious faith. Questioning and challenging conventional perceptions of great historical figures in this type of play is part of what modern playwrights always struggle to do. In fact, it is central to the spirit of modernism. It's what makes the play exciting.

But it has nothing to do with causality in the way I'm using the word here.

Here, I use *causality* to mean *scientifically verifiable* causality.

This other type of cause—More's religious wavering—which appears to bring on the protagonist's problems, is not *causality* at all; it is *morality*.

Bolt's play challenges us, then, to trust in God in ways many Americans at the beginning of the twenty-first century simply are not prepared to do. It is a part of Christian moral teaching that has become a major feature of Western culture. This kind of Christian moral order—that good deeds lead to good consequences, that good people are rewarded and bad people are punished, and that we suffer only when we transgress—is at the heart of a great deal of the most popular epic dramas. Certainly its presence in the movies is self-evident, but even the stage is full of this kind of morality. Take for example the Alain Boublil script for *Les Misérables*. Jean Valjean suffers first because he has stolen a loaf of bread and later because he breaks the law by destroying his parolee documents. The skill in the Boublil script—and in the story provided by Victor Hugo, of course—is in constructing transgressions that, under the circumstances, seem reasonable, even logical.

But Valjean has broken the law and that is the source of his hard life. Fantine also commits a moral error when she resorts to prostitution. So do the students of Paris in starting their rebellion. But they are still good people who are guilty only of errors in judgment. Because they continue to try to do the right thing, they are all rewarded in the end as spirits—in heaven, as it were—joined together for the final song.

But you, the playwright, are not confined to employing this essentially conventional type of moral framework in your epic play.

Tony Kushner certainly wasn't.

In *Angels in America*, right and wrong are not determined by conventional teachings. A more complex moral order has been put in its place. In Kushner's world, being a good man does not hinge on being religious—Joe must abandon his religion to find his own goodness. Nor does being a good man hinge on seeking enlightenment or having compassion—Louis and Belize have those qualities yet are not singled out for the kind of special treatment that awaits Prior Walter.

In Kushner's view of the cosmos, to be a good man is to be a gay man who accepts his gayness, who has been singled out to suffer the collective curse of AIDS, and who suffers it nobly, never retreating from his beliefs, from his sense of humor, or from the literate civilized culture of the urban homosexual community.

That is a good man. A man so good he has been singled out by heaven to be the harbinger of redemption for all of us. A man who speaks to angels.

In the final analysis, there is no tight logical chain of events that makes *inevitable* the climactic blessing delivered to Prior Walter at the end of the play. Prior Walter's happiness is caused by his basic goodness, period. Kushner's genius is in creating a world in which we agree with him, in which we share his vision of life, without ever having been preached to once.

Every effective playwright working in the epic style chooses his or her own overarching moral order to govern the outcome of those unknowable events, setbacks, and plot twists. Yours will probably not be the same as Tony Kushner's. But that is the thing that will give power and authority to your script.

Summary of the Epic Vision

In the epic vision, we express the belief that the world is a complex, sprawling place where we can never anticipate the causes of events, but where we can be confident some sort of moral order will prevail. In the following outline, you will find summarized the key characteristics of that form. As in every chapter, I have used an outline to keep the text distilled and convenient. Use this list as a loose set of guidelines, not as a rigorous table of mathematical formulae.

Action Structure in an Epic Play

The epic form uses an action structure. That is to say, it dramatizes change triggered by knowable causes. But unlike realism, action can also be triggered both by coincidence and by forces outside the words and deeds of the characters.

1. The majority of scenes will show a change occurring in the lives of the characters. However, not all scenes have to do this.

2. Many important changes will be caused by the words and deeds of the characters in the play, but not all of them.

3. Some changes will also be caused by outside forces, such as natural disasters, war, or social upheaval. A coincidental intersection of events might also cause the change. However, these types of changes should be moderated in the following ways:

   • They should be kept to a minimum. The audience's tolerance for coincidence or acts of God tends to be low.

   • They should be constructed to emulate some sort of moral order that the author has chosen to govern the overall outcome of the events in the play.

   • They should tend to reflect an accurate sense of the way in which the world works. They should not be wildly improbable or wholly unexpected occurrences. In other words, the outbreak of war should be hinted at in earlier scenes, the flood should be preceded by a period of torrential rainfall, and so on.

4. Most of the changes that occur in individual scenes will trigger larger, more significant changes in the subsequent scenes—but unlike realism, not all of them have to.

5. After the largest change—the climax—we should get a glimpse of what life will now be like for the characters and the world they inhabit.

The action structure noted here provides the fundamental underpinning of the epic vision. But additional features of epic structure are what truly characterize this form of playwriting. Use of these features has led to the writing of powerful and important epic drama by playwrights like Peter Shaffer, Robert Bolt, David Henry Hwang, and others. Even die-hard realists like Ibsen, Shaw, and Williams were drawn to the epic style from time to time. It is a unique and potent vision, that can empower the playwright to say things in a way not possible in any other dramatic form.

6. Because of the large number of wide-ranging locales, an epic play will often use a narrator. He or she will address the audience in an opening prologue and return, between the scenes, on other occasions.

   • The narrator can be a character from the play who steps outside the story to establish the setting or to explain a transition in time. This character can be the protagonist or a minor character.
   • The narrator can be the entire company of actors, speaking as a chorus.
   • The narrator may not be a character at all. He or she may simply narrate and do nothing more.

7. Scenes tend to be episodic. They do not have to flow from a causal chain of events.

   • Unlike realism, each scene does not have to be caused directly by a preceding scene.

- The order of the scenes can be determined by the chronology of the events or the requirements of the play's themes.
- In any event, the order of the scenes is chosen to achieve the maximum effect of juxtaposing the revelations contained within them.

8. There will be multiple stories unfolding at the same time.

   - These stories will share some characters in common.
   - Characters in any given story line may not even be aware of the existence of the principal characters in the other story lines.
   - Events occurring in one story line will typically have an impact on characters in another story line.

9. There will typically be a large number of characters. Many of these characters will appear in only one or two scenes, thus allowing the same actor to play several roles.

   - Only principal characters must be fully developed, with complex emotional and intellectual lives.
   - Many of the characters may exist only to serve one or two functions in the plot, then never return.
   - Not every character has to have a full story or change in any way.

10. A moral order of some sort must govern the proceedings and ultimately determine who has a happy ending and who doesn't.

Important note: The more complex and challenging this moral order is, the more potent and engaging your play will be.

Background to the Development of Epic Construction

For most of the recorded history of drama, writing in the epic manner was considered heresy. It was virtually forbidden by the French Academy in the seventeenth century, for example, and at least one famous playwright was actually put on trial under suspicion of writing in this style. Shakespeare was criticized by his contemporaries in part because he wrote in an epic style, and the term *upstart crow* was coined as an insult, hurled by one of those critics.

The problem goes back to the Greek philosopher Aristotle.

Around about 330 B.C., Aristotle wrote the first book analyzing drama and what makes it tick. Aristotle's *Poetics* has, to this very day, remained the single most important volume ever composed on the subject, full of important, indispensable truths about the dynamics of creating drama.

But in his little book (it may actually just be a collection of notes from lectures, not a fully fleshed-out treatise), Aristotle goes to great pains to distinguish between dramatic form and epic form. And the epic, he states, is not suitable for the stage. In addition to this, he clearly states that good drama does not narrate stories; it enacts scenes before our eyes.

Greek drama—as with much of Greek culture in general—was preserved for posterity by the Romans, and the debt we owe to those world conquerors is immeasurable. Without the Roman love of all things Greek, we in the twenty-first century would have little knowledge of the Greeks at all. So it's not surprising to discover that serious Roman dramatists also adhered to Aristotle's guidelines, and in so doing, preserved them as the standard of playwriting for centuries. This was despite the fact that Roman audiences much preferred the epic spectacle of re-created battles on land and sea that were regularly staged in great amphitheaters like the Colosseum.

When Rome fell in 476, most of Western Europe lost all contact with classical Greek and Roman notions of art. (In the East, governed from what is now the modern city of Istanbul, classical civilization survived, but theatre did not. It was banned by the Greek Orthodox Church.)

As a result, Western Europeans reinvented drama from scratch. For nearly a thousand years, drama flourished with little or no regard to the standards that had been established by Aristotle.

It was during this period that the groundwork was laid for epic drama as we practice it today. Medieval people had a love of sprawling, epic plays that often took all day to perform. *The Castle of Perseverance* is one of these. A shorter, more manageable play using epic construction is the famous *Everyman*. But even while these morality plays were flourishing, another type of complex dramatic storytelling was developing: the mystery cycles. These dramas typically covered the entire history of the human race, from Creation to Judgment Day, required the use of an entire town to stage their elaborate scenes, and lasted for days on end.

There can be little doubt that it was the mystery cycles that inspired Christopher Marlowe and the sixteenth-century Elizabethans to devise techniques by which a vast, complex story unfolding over many years in many locales could be presented within the confines of an inn yard or a small stage. Though Shakespeare did not invent this dramatic structure, he was the most famous and most brilliant practitioner of it. The epic style survives as a legitimate dramatic form today due more to the soaring genius of his work than to any other single factor. Age after age, when playwrights yearn to express an epic vision of life onstage, it is Shakespeare they cite, Shakespeare they study, and Shakespeare who legitimizes their efforts.

However, on the European continent, scholars had in the meantime rediscovered the treatises written about drama by Aristotle, Horace and even Plato, who felt drama should be banned altogether. Electrified by these insights into dramatic art, scholars and classically educated playwrights set out to write for themselves drama that would rival the fame and majesty of ancient Greek drama. These new/old ideas about how plays should be written spread across Europe but took root most successfully in France. There, inspired by Aristotle's ideas, brilliant writers like Molière and Racine created timeless drama in the classical style: a small cast of characters, one location, one story line, and a series of events that unfolds within a single day. Backed by the French Academy, these neoclassicists asserted that all *real* plays, all *good* plays were written in this manner. The other types of plays—the ones that Marlowe and Shakespeare wrote—were corrupt and exerted a bad influence on society.

For a long time the neoclassicists were triumphant. When the Puritans seized control of England in 1642, the theatre of Shakespeare and Marlowe was shut down forever. All that remained were the French and Italian models of drama, and they remained the standard of good playwriting for more than a century.

But at the end of the eighteenth century, the classical standards of dramatic writing were challenged once more. And ultimately it was melodrama—citing Shakespeare as its model—that put the popular epic back on the stage once and for all.

5

Brecht and an
Alternative Epic

What about this idea, then, that we can take action
and change the world? Is it really possible? That
I, who am not a powerful politician or a corpo-
rate leader or a wealthy investor, can actually in my own
humble way do things that will have a meaningful effect on
the world around me?

This notion seems to fly in the face of reality, given the
world we live in. And recent history has subjected us to
experiences that directly contradict the idea that we can
change the world in any way.

Beginning with the Industrial Revolution and the relo-
cation of masses of workers from the countryside to the city,
modern history has demonstrated how helpless we really
are. In Scotland, people's homes were burned to the ground,
forcing them into the cities, while in other parts of Europe,
the land was simply bought up from under them. Once they
were relocated in the great new industrial centers, their lives
were at the disposal of the factory owners and managers.
An exhausted man on the assembly line could be replaced

in a heartbeat by one of hundreds begging for jobs at the factory gate. Industrial accidents were commonplace, even for children, who were employed doing work that required small hands and bodies, such as cleaning machinery in difficult-to-reach places. Medical services were scant and expensive, and those who were unable to work crammed into wretched dormitories called workhouses.

The loss of autonomy and dignity that began during the Industrial Revolution escalated with the outbreak of World War I. Trench warfare required the massing of thousands upon thousands of young men in what were often brutally primitive conditions. They were sacrificed in pointless, suicidal assaults on heavily defended machine gun and artillery positions. At the Battle of the Somme, more than a million men died. England alone suffered five hundred thousand casualties in one battle.

And after the Great War, people were hurled into the Great Depression. Again, whole populations were gripped by events over which they had no control, unable to provide basic food and shelter for themselves and their families, much less have any effect on the world around them. The notion that individual human beings can take action and change things would have seemed a laughable proposition.

Into this state of crisis strode a brilliant young dramatist, Bertolt Brecht. Brecht had a vision of life that gave new hope to the idea that change is possible. And he came up with an approach to theatre that would empower him to share that vision with the world. Along the way, he invented important new approaches to writing and staging plays that provide you and me, at the start of the new century, with tools and techniques that can galvanize an audience and instill our theatre with power.

The dramatic techniques Brecht developed literally changed forever what is now possible for a playwright to envision onstage.

Brecht understood that the world is a place in which any change that occurs is most likely to be a result of the intersection of other people's lives with ours, unfolding over a long period of time in many different places.

So he turned to epic structure to express his particular vision of life.

But the epic structure he had inherited from nineteenth-century melodrama—and even to some extent, from Shakespeare—would not suffice. These were epic plays that he believed simply served to distract the audience from the world around them; they're diversions and entertainments. Instead, he wanted his audiences to focus on the world, to learn about the world, and to begin to see exactly what forces shape and control their lives.

People can produce change, Brecht believed, but only when we achieve two goals:

- We must be given the opportunity to learn exactly what is making us miserable.
- We must be motivated to go out *as a group* to improve the world.

Meaningful change can never be produced by individuals acting on their own. Yes, it might *seem* that individuals have produced change, but if they've appeared to alter the world, it is usually in an inconsequential way or in a way that is quickly reversed by the greater powers around us.

To illustrate this point that the change we produce as individuals is either illusory or nonexistent, Brecht made the scenes in his plays all reflect this truth about life. He knew that the best way to communicate a message to an audience is by showing, not preaching, so he made all of the elements of his plays interact in the same way he believed the world itself operates.

In *The Caucasian Chalk Circle*, for example, various characters at various times initiate actions that produce change. A revolution occurs. A tyrant escapes. Two young people discover love. But those changes are quickly canceled out. The rebels are overthrown. The tyrant is captured. The lovers are torn apart. The final change at the end of the play occurs when the young woman Grusha is made the legal mother of the abandoned child she has sheltered throughout the story, even when the biological mother returns to claim him. But that change is the result of an extraordinary series of coincidences. The one person in the entire kingdom who would understand that Grusha has the stronger claim to the child—the former clerk, Azdak—is appointed to be judge only because of wild improbabilities. He is a liar, a con artist, and a drunkard, and he accepts bribes regularly, all the time subverting the law in clever ways so that justice, as he sees it, can be administered regardless of what the law really says. In other words, the only man capable of rendering true justice is unfit by conventional standards to be a judge. And as soon as Azdak renders his verdict, he knows he must run and hide before he is forcibly removed from office. So although Grusha is declared to be the mother of the child she loves and cherishes, justice itself is shown to be ephemeral. No judge who administers true justice will ever be allowed to remain in office.

Even though an individual has produced change, it is temporary. The status quo is restored. The system lumbers on, unaltered.

Brecht uses *The Good Person of Setzuan* to show the world in an even more cynical light. The prostitute Shen Te is given gold from the gods so that she can give up whoring and open a tobacco shop. But she has to invent a hard-hearted alter ego, her fictitious cousin Mr. Shui Ta, to collect debts and enforce good business practices. It seems

Shen Te has solved her problem—until she falls in love. Once again, her basic goodness betrays her and the young man cons her out of all her money. By the end of the play, nothing has changed. The impossibility of being a good person in the world as it presently exists is potently illustrated. Even the gods themselves are helpless to solve the problem.

Brecht's greatest work is probably *Mother Courage and Her Children*. It is certainly among his bleakest and most powerful plays. It shows us a hardened, worldly woman, Anna Fearling, who knows that in order to provide for herself and her three children she has to place practical considerations above emotional needs. Money buys food. Noble, self-sacrificing actions don't. The world in which Mother Courage operates is one of never-ending war, and she survives by selling supplies to the soldiers. At the start of the play, she has her two sons and her mute daughter working with her. Her twin goals are to keep her children out of the war and at the same time make the hardheaded business deals she must in order to survive. Time after time these goals are in direct opposition to each other. Her willingness to be a friendly businesswoman with the soldiers gives her first son the opportunity to sneak off and join the army. When her second son is accused of stealing from one of the armies, she can only save his life by selling her wagon, but she haggles over the price too long. And while she is away doing business in town, her third child sacrifices her own life to save innocent villagers. On each occasion, we think Mother Courage is going to see the light of day, that she will finally learn to put her children before her profits. Yet in each case she refuses to change. Brecht's point is that in war, everyone loses, including the profiteers. That much is clear on the most obvious thematic level.

But on a subtler level, Brecht's world rings true to us because he is showing us something we have always secretly suspected to be true: nothing changes.

People don't change.

The world doesn't change.

Life doesn't change.

Brecht tantalizes us with the *possibility* of change but shows that in the end any improvement or enlightenment achieved by individual human beings is illusory.

Only when we recognize this can we begin to look for true change. And true change can only be produced by people working together as a group.

Brecht created a theatre to teach us exactly this, a theatre in which almost no change actually occurs to the *characters*, but one in which the *audience* learns so much from the ideas and the situations presented that it is motivated to go out and take action, as a group.

In the case of *Mother Courage*, for example, Brecht wanted us to learn about the futility and misery of war and so encourage us collectively to resist war, to not be deluded by the promises and the rhetoric of the military machine. In *The Good Person of Setzuan,* he wanted us to learn about the evils of traditional business as well as the clash between our core humanist values and the demands of "good business practices." In this way, he wanted to encourage us to soften our insistence on the hardened rules of capitalism. He also hoped to pave the way for more radical changes—the instituting of social programs and the dismantling of private business altogether.

Whether or not you agree with Brecht's political goals is beside the point. If you believe that the theatre can teach important things about the world—thus motivating us to go out and change the world—Brecht's techniques can be vitally important to capturing your vision onstage.

To accomplish this, to create theatre in which the audience actually learns the truth about the world, you must first be willing to make it less of a diversion, less of an escapist entertainment.

But once you've done that, what will hold your audience's attention? If people don't enjoy your play, why on earth would they watch it?

Brecht believed they will enjoy your play because, above all, people enjoy learning. It's one of life's greatest pleasures, and if we are *learning* while watching a play, we will be enthralled by it. But in order to free up our learning abilities, Brecht asserted, you have to keep us from getting carried away by our emotions.

This in and of itself was a radical departure from anything anyone had ever attempted in the theatre before.

Typically, when a playwright wants to get an audience deeply involved in the action of a play, he or she will create emotionally charged situations that keep the audience members on the edges of their seats. But Brecht believed that you're cheating the audience when you do this. Emotion-based theatre will always be an inferior type of drama, according to him, because an audience emotionally immersed in a play is by and large not capable of learning anything. Learning requires that the intellect be alive and engaged, and emotions tend to cancel out our ability to reflect on things.

The most fundamental trick we use in the theatre when we want to stimulate an audience's emotions is *illusion*. This is why so much energy is lavished on realistic scenery; to give the illusion that the audience is really there. That is why writers rewrite and polish dialogue to make it flow naturally and easily: to give the illusion that these are real conversations. And that is why most actors dedicate years of training to master the skills of behavior and psychology: to create the illusion that their characters are real people.

In Brecht's theatre, all of these illusions are smashed.

To begin with, there is no traditional scenery. In fact, his plays will often be produced on a bare stage with the curtains removed so that the fixtures and brick walls are clearly visible to the audience. When the scene requires a house, three crude sticks assembled like a doorway might be used instead. If the scene takes place by a river, two actors will stand in full view of the audience and create waves by holding a long stretch of rough blue cloth.

Similarly, Brecht believed that the script should be written in a way that constantly reminds us we are in the theatre, watching a play. He believed that playwrights should stop trying to make audiences feel as if the events of the story are actually happening in front of them for the first time. He advised writers to never let the audience forget that the events and the characters in the play are an artificial construct put together by an author with a specific purpose in mind. To accomplish this, Brecht himself uses a variety of techniques to interrupt the action and to pull us out of the story. For example, his plays will call for the use of placards presented at the start of a scene or in the middle of a scene, giving away the plot or calling our attention to the moral lesson being taught. Characters will sing songs that have nothing to do with the plot. Narration will be used to interrupt the flow of the story.

He called on actors to approach their work in the same way. Don't lose yourself in the character, he told his actors, but always remain present as yourself, commenting on the actions and words of the script with your tone of voice or a raised eyebrow. The audience should always be aware that the characters onstage are not real people. They are illusions created by men and women with their own thoughts and beliefs who have specific ideas about what the audience should learn from the play.

And once the audience has been freed from the emotional seduction of traditional entertainment, it will pay attention to the ideas being transmitted by the playwright.

But of all Brecht's dramatic innovations, the one most certain to make an audience want to leave the theatre and produce change in the world is his brilliant implementation of the central edict of modern art: never give the audience an answer to the problem you have presented.

No other writer in the modern period has carried this dictum to the extreme that Brecht did.

In his plays he makes a point of convincing us that both sides of the question are absolutely irrefutable. By doing this, he consciously creates a clash between equally valid ideas in the audience's mind. And he never gives the audience an answer to the paradox. We see that old people and poverty-stricken people need assistance or they will perish before our eyes; yet at the same time we see that good business practices prevent us from helping them. That a mother who must buy and sell goods to provide for her children cannot ignore her business to watch out for them, or mother and child alike will starve.

From this clash of equally valid ideas, he hoped that a discussion would occur among members of the audience.

And from this discussion, or *dialectic*, the audience would arrive at the truth on its own.

Summary of the Brechtian Epic

In the Brechtian epic, we express many of the same beliefs that lie at the heart of the mainstream epic: the world is a complex place where we can never anticipate the causes of events. But where, in the mainstream epic, we can be confident some sort of moral order will prevail, in Brecht's world this does not hold true. Instead, we know we will witness insoluble problems and individual characters who cannot produce substantive change as long as they operate as individuals. In the following outline, you will find summarized the key characteristics of the Brechtian epic.

Action Structure in the Brechtian Epic

The basic dynamics of action are sometimes utilized in this form and sometimes not. That is to say, in some scenes, characters will take actions that cause change, but since the point of the Brechtian vision is that people operating alone cannot change the world, it is more typical to see the characters' actions altering nothing in the world around them.

1. It is most typical of this approach to writing plays that characters undertake action that produces no change. Instead, the audience's attention is held by the clash of irreconcilable ideas.

2. When changes do occur, they are most likely to be caused by outside forces, such as war or social upheaval, or by a coincidental intersection of people's lives, not by the actions of individuals.

3. When the words and deeds of the characters do produce change, those changes should be temporary or illusory, that is to say, they are easily undone or revealed to have never actually occurred.

4. So long as this "temporary and illusory" principle is observed, changes that occur in individual scenes can cause other changes in the subsequent scenes.

5. At the climax of the play, however, there should be no change at all. Instead, we should be left in the grips of forces struggling to produce change but unable to do so.

These points summarize the role of action structure in the Brechtian epic. But they do not constitute the heart of what Brecht was trying to accomplish onstage. Nor would they be considered the signature features of the Brechtian style. To truly utilize Brecht's innovations, other features will need to appear in your script. Many of these have become commonplace in the American theatre. They have been adapted and used in plays and musicals as unexpected as *Our Town*, *The Fantastiks*, and *Pippin*. The key is to remember that your goal is to enhance the audience's learning experience, not find a low-budget way to divert it from its problems.

Brecht believed that a play would only be instructive if it used the simplest type of epic structure—scenes that unfold in their most basic chronological order, rather than in the manner of a cleverly constructed plot. Brecht also searched for as many ways as possible to interrupt the play, thus keeping the audience's emotional involvement at a low pitch and its intellectual engagement high.

6. Seek to destroy illusion on the stage. Use only the most minimal scenery, and construct it to look false. Costumes should look as if they were assembled from secondhand castoffs. Props should be simple and crude.

7. Interrupt the smooth flow of the story by having characters stop to tell unrelated anecdotes or sing unrelated songs. Another way to do this is to write speeches that call for your actors to break out of character and speak directly to the audience as themselves.

8. Use placards, or crudely executed slide projections, to give away key developments in the plot. They

can also draw the audience's attention to the moral point of the scene.

9. Never use narration to enhance the audience's suspension of disbelief or to help it imagine the scene better. Instead, use narration to interrupt the flow of the story.

10. Always try to show the audience familiar things in unexpected ways. Using unexpected objects as props or using the theatre space in unexpected ways, for example, reminds audiences they are *in* the theatre. This, in and of itself, stimulates their intellects in an enjoyable way as well as making them partners in the creation of the play.

Background to the Development of Brecht's Theatre

Since the beginning, drama has typically been a process of stimulating an audience's emotions. Although the Greeks placed great emphasis on intellectual reflection and the pre-eminence of the mind over emotions, Aristotle wrote that the purpose of drama was to provoke pity and fear in an audience, and by so doing, purge the audience of these feelings.

In fact, Plato wrote in *The Republic* that theatre should be banned outright, in part because it puts us in a highly charged emotional state.

At the end of the eighteenth century, when theatre was deemed in need of a complete overhaul—along with the rest of art— it was because it had strayed too far from emotions and had, under the rigors of neoclassicism, become a cold, intellectual exercise. The playwrights of the Sturm und

Drang school, as well as the romantic movement in general, sought to put the emotions back into theatre. They probably went overboard in their efforts. But the dramatic form that replaced their efforts, melodrama, was just as saturated with emotional excess.

Ultimately, melodrama would yield to realism and naturalism, but both of those depended on essentially melodramatic plots that were simply told with greater skill and held to more rigorous standards.

Bertolt Brecht (1898–1956) is considered the most important dramatic theorist since Aristotle in part because he is the first playwright to challenge the assumptions of emotion-based theatre and offer a viable alternative. His reasons for doing so are no secret. Like Karl Marx, Brecht believed it was only a matter of time until the natural course of events would force common workers everywhere to organize themselves and establish collective ownership of all businesses. More likely than not, this would be achieved by violent revolution. Brecht's Marxist rhetoric is well-known.

We are often less familiar with the fact that Brecht was never really able to conform to Marxism himself. As a result, he was continually criticized by Communist authorities and fellow Marxists for failing to adhere to Party rhetoric in his works. After *Mother Courage* was performed in Berlin, hard-line Party members claimed that Brecht had sold short the cause. In their minds, Anna Fearling should have been transformed into a political activist by her experiences.

But Brecht's innate grasp of the complexity and frailty of the human spirit was too strong to ever allow him to cooperate with such ham-handed orthodoxy. Especially in his later career, his plays reflected a genuine feeling for the needs of common people everywhere, and his astonishing ability to capture the reality of ordinary lives onstage always won out over whatever formal lesson he may have set out to teach us.

It is Brecht's focus on the individual human spirit that has won him his position among the ranks of great humanist playwrights. His innovations in dramatic form and structure, as well as the changes in staging technique that make his plays so distinctive, place him in the company of the world's greatest dramatic theorists.

For playwrights who have a vision that change is possible in the modern world, Brecht can be a truly important source of empowering ideas.

6

Afternote

A Few Words from Realism, the Epic, and Brecht

There is no particular reason why ideas have to be explained with difficult language. If the theorist or teacher investigating an idea has a passion for communication and a willingness to probe into an idea until its simplest, most commonly understood elements are revealed, then a great deal of awkward jargon can be disposed of. But even jargon-free language should be used precisely. Words within a particular area of study, which are also used in general conversation, can have distinctly different meanings depending on the context in which they're used.

For example, if I say something is realistic in general conversation, I am probably praising its close similarity to real life. But if I call a play realistic, it means something very different. In dramatic art, anything that even roughly resembles reality can be called realistic. To say within the context of dramatic art that something has a close similarity to real life, the word *naturalistic* would be more accurate. Though related to realism, naturalism is a distant cousin and constitutes a whole new model of reality, which we'll examine in a subsequent chapter.

To help the working playwright who seeks to acquire an effective command of theoretical language, at the end of each major section in this book there will be a summary of some of the key words used in that section. Each summary will include tips on how to avoid common pitfalls when using specific words that are liable to be misinterpreted.

Realism

In everyday use, the word realism means different things from its strict definition in dramatic art. As a result, some confusion can develop around the use of this word and words related to it. This confusion is redoubled if the playwright has experience in literary criticism, for there, *realism* means "slice of life," something it does *not* mean in dramatic literature.

The three words to watch out for are *realist*, *realistic*, and *naturalist*. They do not mean the same thing and in dramatic art they are not interchangeable.

Realistic refers to any play that resembles reality.

Realist refers to plays that are contrived to reflect the underlying cause-to-effect nature of the world. The realist play adheres more or less to the strictures laid out in Chapter 3. It is scientific and objective, primarily in its attitude toward causality.

Naturalist refers to plays that reproduce the world in all its messy details onstage—a world dominated and controlled by heredity and the environment.

Naturalist plays also try to be scientific, but in a very different way from realist plays. Naturalism, in fact, grew out of people's frustrated reaction against the optimistic belief that we can produce change in the world around us. The naturalist playwriting form is used to express the vision that, yes, we can know the causes of our problems, but we can't ever solve them.

This approach to playwriting will be examined in Part Three, "A Vision of Futility."

The Epic

In general usage, the word *epic* summons up associations with historical material as well as suggesting material that has a sweeping scope to it. In the dramatist's language, however, *epic* does not mean either of these things. If we mistakenly assume that an epic play has something to do with history, we would certainly cite Robert Bolt's *A Man for All Seasons*, Peter Shaffer's *Amadeus*, Bertolt Brecht's *Galileo*, and George Bernard Shaw's *Caesar and Cleopatra* as examples of that particular style.

Obviously, these are costume dramas set in another historical period. But that feature is not what makes them epic. In fact, historical costume dramas can be written with whatever vision is most truthful to the playwright. *The Lion in Winter* is a realist costume drama, as is Shaw's *Man of Destiny*. *The Lark* is a costume drama about Joan of Arc written as existentialist drama. *Rosencrantz and Guildenstern Are Dead* is an absurdist costume drama.

If a costume drama is written with a sweeping scope, *then* is it an epic? Not necessarily.

Yes, epic plays are set in many different locales over an extended period of time, but to most people, "sweeping scope" means more than that. When we say something has sweeping scope, we generally assume the subject matter will be of monumental importance—history-making people engaged in earth-shattering issues that involve the rise and fall of nations, the survival or loss of many lives, revolution, and war. And though an epic play can have those qualities, it might also be as ordinary and simple as one man coming to terms with the real nature of love, as in Tom Stoppard's *The Real Thing*.

In order for a play to be epic in the context of dramatic literature, it must use the structural devices outlined in Chapter 4, and it must use them as a means of expressing the belief that the world is a sprawling, complex place that is only partially governed by causality—a place where, in the end, some kind of moral order will prevail.

Another word has recently come into use to describe this style of writing: *extensive*. That is to say, an extensive (or epic) play *extends* over a long period of time, multiple locations, and so on. It is used in contrast with the word *intensive*. An intensive play—that is, a classical or realist play—is compressed into the minimum number of characters and locations and a short, *intense* period of time.

Although using the word *extensive* deprives us of an inherent reminder that this writing style derives from Shakespeare, medieval mystery cycles, and a literary tradition that dates back to Homer, it does have a clean, clear feeling to it. It frees us from the inaccurate association between epic structure and plays that are simply set in another historical period. That by itself may make it easier for the playwright to understand how to use this technique to bring his or her own vision of life to the stage.

The Brechtian Epic

The study of Brecht and his contribution to theatre is an area to which you could devote your entire life. The brief insight into some of Brecht's ideas that I have attempted to share here is in no way meant to deter the serious playwright from an in-depth examination of the man and his work. But there are two words that usually come up when dealing with Brecht that even the most cursory introduction should address, and it is my intention to do so now.

Almost everyone who has had contact with Brecht's plays or theories has heard of the *alienation effect*. In German, the word Brecht used was *verfremdungseffekt*. English, however, is poorly equipped to capture the ideas that can be densely assembled in a single German word, and when we translate *verfremdung* as alienation, we are inadvertently doing Brecht a disservice.

The misunderstanding that often stems from this inaccurate translation is the notion that Brecht's theatrical techniques were intended to push the audience away, to disengage it from the theatrical experience, in a word, to alienate it.

The last thing Brecht wanted was to alienate his audience.

His intention, rather, was to prevent us from turning off our brains and getting caught up in the emotions of the story. He does this by continually showing the audience people, objects, and events in the most unfamiliar ways possible. His goal is to keep us from falling into habitual responses as we watch the play unfold.

Verfremdungseffekt means exactly this: making stage events so strange, so unexpected, that the audience will be stimulated and provoked into asking questions.

The second word that comes up when we study Brecht is *dialectic*. Specifically, students of dramatic art will hear or read about Brecht's use of a dialectical structure. A full explanation of that concept is beyond the scope of this book, but some clarification can be provided here.

Among philosophers, the word *dialectic* means an argument or a discussion based on opposing views. Use of the word in this sense is as old as Plato. But in the nineteenth century, the German philosopher G. W. F. Hegel used the word in a new way. Hegel believed that truth is arrived at through a process of dialectical conflicts that occur in our thoughts as we observe the world around us. No concept can exist, according to Hegel, without the simultaneous and inescapable assumption that it also does *not* exist.

For example, we know what a table is first of all by differentiating between *that which is table* and *that which is not table*. These two absolutely contradictory states—being and not being—clash, and the result is that we now understand a table to be something with limited existence. Sometimes it exists, sometimes it doesn't. How? Simply because before it was built, it didn't exist. And after enough time goes by, it will cease to exist. In other words, we can make sense of something both existing and not existing by observing that it exists at some times and at other times does not.

Gradually, in this way, we arrive at a more complete idea of what a table is and how it figures into our world. This is called a Hegelian dialectic.

We begin with a thesis, which automatically and of necessity has an antithesis.

They collide, and fuse, and create a synthesis—a new entity that possesses the qualities of both.

The synthesis becomes the new thesis, which automatically and of necessity has an antithesis.

Again, they fuse, and the process repeats itself until, in Hegel's view, we arrive at the truth.

When we say Brecht uses a dialectical structure in his plays, then, we mean to a large extent that he is following this model. He presents ideas that are diametrically opposite to each other—a thesis and an antithesis—in the hope that the audience will provide a synthesis.

7

Naturalism

The belief that any meaningful change in this world will ever occur in our lifetimes is, of course, an illusion. What makes that realization especially disturbing is the recognition that the realists were at least partly right: We *can* know the causes of our problems.

We just can't do anything to change them.

This, at least, is the point of view held by many who see the world with what I call a vision of futility. And, frankly, they may be right. One of the first dramatic forms created to express this vision of life onstage was naturalism. Although in the beginning, the naturalists were probably somewhat optimistic in their outlook, believing that by approaching life in a certain way we might make this world a better place, the truth soon overtook them with shattering finality: You can do all the elaborate sociological and psychological studies you want. In the end, there are two things that determine who we are and how we live:

- environment
- heredity.

Certainly it is obvious that the environment in which we are raised determines much of our surface behavior. Our social manners, our ideas about personal hygiene and diet, even our ways of speaking are all shaped by the milieu in which we are immersed as children. And all of these things affect our ability to get ahead in the world, to meet new people, to be exposed to opportunities.

Even if these things are unlearned or corrected, there are far deeper ways in which the milieu of our childhood has shaped us—our values, our expectations of ourselves and others, our self-esteem or lack thereof—and all of these defining assumptions remain with us, unaltered, until the day we die.

In addition to having to cope with our environment, we are also saddled with heredity. And the emerging science of genetics has only confirmed the importance of bloodlines in determining who we are and how we behave. Breakthroughs continue to occur in rapid succession confirming that sociopathic behavior, obesity, susceptibility to disease, depression, and abusive behavior are all encoded in our genes long before we're born.

In naturalism, then, the characters are shown to be in the grip of these powerful forces.

Let's take a look at heredity. Arthur Miller's masterpiece *Death of a Salesman* is essentially a realist play, but in it, Miller draws heavily on this aspect of naturalism as he explores the fate of an archetypal American family. Although Willy Loman is a devoted, hardworking father, we learn he has a powerful womanizing streak in him. Still, Willy continues to slave away at a thankless job in the belief that eventually it will bring success and material security to himself and his family. At an early age, his brother Ben went a different route. Ben, it seems, severed himself from conventional life, went into the world, made a fortune, and became a ghost of regret that has tormented Willy ever since.

Willy now has two sons, Biff and Hap, and in these boys we see the genetic legacy of the Loman family reasserting itself. Biff is the most physically active, most dynamic of the two, and seemingly the one with the most promise. But Biff's interest in success was destroyed when he discovered that his father was cheating on his mother. Ultimately, it is Biff who will break away from conventional middle-class life and go into the world to seek his fortune, and so we get a glimpse of what probably drove Ben away from his and Willy's father all those years ago.

Meanwhile, Hap has inherited the womanizing genes of the family. Yet upon Willy's death, it is Hap who dedicates himself to getting married and achieving the conventional success that always eluded his father. It doesn't take much imagination to see, years from now, Hap's weakness for women being discovered by his own son and another disillusioned boy being driven away from his family—heredity proving once again that we are not really in control of our own destinies at all.

In John Millington Synge's *The Playboy of the Western World*, we see an example of characters whose lives are shaped by their environment. In fact, environment so dominates the play that it cannot be understood or performed well without a strong grasp of the realities of rural Irish life, especially in the western part of that country. Isolation from the European mainstream, chronic economic depression, and gloomy weather collectively function like a real character in the play, as real as the protagonists Christy Mahon and Pegeen Mike. These are the bleak environmental realities that often lead to a kind of spiritual unhappiness that can be seen to overtake people in any part of the world subjected to similar conditions. If there is a cultural willingness to wink at alcohol consumption used to ease the pain, you have all the basic ingredients for domestic violence. These are the conditions that dictate Christy Mahon's life to him. When he raises his shovel to kill his abusive father while they're working together in the fields, he is following a course of rebellion as predestined as Oedipus'—a course shaped for him by the realities of the world around him, not by his own free will.

The play is, of course, a comedy. But underneath the laughter, the audience experiences general horror, both at what Christy has done and the fact that the inhabitants of a remote village turn him into a local hero for having done it. At least, they do until Christy's father shows up, bleeding and bandaged, to make them face the reality of what the hotheaded boy attempted to do, at which point they, too, turn on Christy in horror. This new environmental reality propels Christy into a life of homeless wandering, again, through no real choice of his own.

The vision of futility, as expressed in naturalism, tells us this: Since environment and heredity cause our problems, and since those two factors can never be changed, our problems can never be solved. As a result, the overriding tone of the naturalist play—in contrast to the realist play—is one of bleak inevitability, even in a play as full of laughter as *The Playboy of the Western World*.

This approach to art first appeared in France in the nineteenth century, and although it saw genuine success in literature and painting, in the theatre it proved harder to capture. Most of the "naturalist" plays of the period were nothing more than traditional melodramas produced with startlingly authentic sets and costumes. Playwrights like Gerhart Hauptmann and Georg Buchner certainly had better luck than the French in capturing the vision of futility in their scripts, but it was the great Russian theatrical pioneers Anton Chekov and Constantin Stanislavski who brought naturalism to life. In their brilliant productions of Chekov's scripts, they formalized the first basic set of techniques necessary for capturing that vision in the theatre.

What is this vision, then?

Naturalism is nothing more or less than the attempt to put life onstage as it actually exists in the world. What Chekov set out to do—what every naturalist does—is create a theatre that represents people without altering them in the slightest way. If at all possible, it calls upon the director, the actors, and the designers to scientifically reproduce onstage each nuance of dress, speech, and mannerism these same people would have in real life. In fact, early naturalists were known for actually moving entire tenement buildings, board by board, onto the stage, because the idea is to show the truth of real life.

But the most important truth of all is this: In real life, nothing ever changes, at least, not in a way we can control or alter.

Our various undertakings may meet with success or failure, but our essential relationships with people, the world in which we move, our prejudices and assumptions, and life for the people around us seldom, if ever, change. Loved ones may die. Jobs may be lost or won. But after an initial rush of emotion—usually experienced only internally by the individual involved—things continue pretty much as they always have.

It was Chekov's notion that, in order to capture this fundamental truth onstage as a writer, you must at all costs avoid "dramatic" confrontations in which characters articulate their problems and solutions are arrived at. To him, the worst kind of "dramatic" playwriting is exemplified by the plays of Henrik Ibsen. Look at the end of Ibsen's *A Doll's House*. Here we witness a scene in which an alienated young wife and mother, Nora, has a full-out confrontation with her well-meaning but insensitive husband. In the course of ten or fifteen minutes, they challenge each other's notions of marriage, law, society, and justice. Nora, of course, reaches her famous conclusion that she must become an adult before she can be a wife or a mother and she leaves her husband in order to learn about the world on her own, as every adult must.

Chekov thought this kind of drama was phony. To his mind, people are never able to heave their thoughts and emotions into their mouths with such clarity and directness. We talk around the subject, often never even realizing what is bothering us. And on the rare occasion when we do insist on an open confrontation, it never really changes anything. Why? Because convincing people we are right is not enough. People are in the grips of far more powerful forces than mere ideas.

Even when, in *Uncle Vanya*, the title character finally confronts his nemesis, Serebryakov, nothing is changed. Economics, heredity, and environment compel Vanya to remain in the same soul-killing position he occupied before the confrontation.

And in his last two plays, Chekov's brilliant evocation of the vision of futility brought him to the recognition that, in life, these confrontations almost never occur. When dramatic events *do* alter the lives of his characters, they happen either offstage where no one can see or between the acts when no one can see. Because the truth is, when events change our lives, we are rarely there to witness them. We are at a party with our friends, we get a phone call from a brother or sister, and so we learn that our parents have decided to get a divorce. We experience sadness, uncertainty, betrayal, but the party goes on, a little differently perhaps, but nothing really changes.

"Let the things that happen onstage be just as complex yet just as simple as they are in life," Chekov wrote. "For instance, people are having a meal at a table, just having a meal, but at the same time their happiness is being created, or their lives are being smashed up . . ." and the phone rings.

Or a friend drops by with a piece of quiet news. And though nothing dramatic has changed at the moment, we know that our happiness has been affected forever.

Note the phrasing: "nothing dramatic has changed at the moment."

Substantive, dramatic plot twists are the kind of change we have been examining here. But conditions in your characters' lives may be altered in tiny, barely visible ways as well.

Although this process of gradual accretion can be loosely described as change, it is not *dramatic change*. Instead, these subtle, slowly accumulating mood shifts reflect a wholly different kind of truth about life:

Gradually, over time, things get worse. Our dreams go unrealized. We get old. Disease sets in. Friends and family pass away.

This is a reality that's wholly different from *dramatic change*, and it's one that naturalism captures extremely well.

In fact, in the naturalist vision, gradual *erosion* is the only development in life that you can truly count on.

Summary of the Naturalist Vision

In the naturalist vision of life, we express the belief that the world is governed by forces over which human beings can never really exert control. These forces are not divine or abstract, like fate or Providence. They are factual and can be confirmed by scientific methods. They work to cancel out any attempt by human beings to produce meaningful change in the world. Conditions can gradually alter in the naturalist vision of life, however, due to the undeniable fact that, over time, things get worse. A summary of key techniques for bringing this vision to the stage follows.

Non-action Structure in a Naturalist Play

Naturalism does not use an action structure. This is extremely important: When characters seek to produce change, they are almost never successful. What minor changes they *do* produce are only on the surface. The underlying condition of their lives is never altered.

1. Characters are shown to be in situations that compel them to want change.

   - The situation might be a painful family environment.
   - It might be an oppressive political situation.
   - It might be a form of social oppression, like racial prejudice or sexism.

2. Some of the characters will be resigned to the situation, but some characters will try to change it.

3. The fact that at least one character seeks to produce change is essential to dynamically illustrating the underlying vision of the play.

4. Those few characters who *do* seek to produce change do so in different ways.

   - Some will be obviously idealistic.
   - Some will be too cynical and ruthless for the audience's taste.
   - Some will appear to have the right balance of realistic thinking and reliable ethics.

5. In some scenes, change will appear to occur or to be imminent. If change *does* occur, it produces consequences that only worsen the lives of the characters.

The great challenge of writing in the naturalist style is to show a world in which the characters can change nothing, and yet somehow prevent the play from being static and boring. Consequently, it is essential to show at least one character attempt to produce change and even seem to produce change, just to keep things interesting. And if change *does* occur, it should fall within the general characteristics noted in the next section.

6. Some changes can be caused by forces we generally recognize to be normal or natural. For example:

   - Someone very old or diseased may, over time, die.
   - A military unit or a government employee may simply be reassigned to another city.
   - An area of the country typically subjected to extreme weather may have to endure an onslaught of snow or rain.
   - People working in jobs with a high turnover rate may simply get fired, for no apparent or substantive reason.

7. Dramatic changes brought about by the actions of characters can occur offstage and be reported by someone who witnessed them, after the audience has already figured out what happened.

8. Dramatic changes that are brought about by the actions of the characters can occur between the acts or scenes. In this case, it is better if no one summarizes the change to the audience. Rather, let the audience members deduce for themselves what happened.

9. One type of permissible change is when the characters are engaged in a technical activity that always

produces change, for example, building something onstage, making and sharing a meal, or cleaning a room.

10. Finally, an important change can occur onstage if something trivial is occupying the audience's attention. For example, patrons in a diner may be arguing loudly about who ate the last piece of pie while, in the corner, a waitress opens her paycheck to discover a pink slip inside.

Background to the Development of Naturalism

This approach to art had its earliest advocate in the French novelist Emile Zola. He believed that, in art, the artificial manipulation of events and characters was unnecessary and untruthful. Simply record the world as it is, he advocated, and you will come closest to the truth. Even to this day, Zola's writings remain extraordinarily powerful testaments to his ideas. More recently, a variation of this approach has appeared in the work of Tom Wolf and Gore Vidal, that is, the "nonfiction" novel.

But what succeeds in a novel may not succeed onstage. This lesson was learned first by producers in France who tried to transfer Zola's ideas to the theatre. Led most famously by André Antoine at the Théatre Libre in Paris, their efforts were important but not especially successful in capturing the naturalist vision.

Then a funny thing happened on the way to the twentieth century.

An obscure Russian playwright, trained as a physician, came to the attention of a prestigious new theatre company in Moscow. Anton Chekov, who had been writing broad comedies about Russian character types, began to author more serious plays and in 1896 achieved his first success in this line with *The Seagull*. It was chosen by Constantin Stanislavski as a vehicle by which his acting company would demonstrate to Russia this powerful new vision of life called naturalism. The irony is that Chekov never saw his plays as slow-moving, portentous dramas. His intention was to write comedy, but Stanislavski's interpretation of his work has set the tone of Chekovian theatre forever. The premiere of *The Seagull* at the Moscow Art Theatre on December 17, 1898, shook the theatre world to its core. What you and I can do on the stage was forever enlarged by the collaboration of these two great men.

After the success of *The Seagull*, they went on to expand and refine their techniques through Chekov's next three plays, and would have, no doubt, continued beyond that. However, Anton Chekov died of tuberculosis in 1904. He was forty-four years old, had only written four major plays, and yet had transformed world drama forever.

In Europe, playwrights like Gerhart Hauptmann and Maxim Gorky continued to refine this new style after Chekov's death. In America, Eugene O'Neill and Elmer Rice wrote great naturalist plays. The Irish theatre saw outstanding naturalist work by Synge and Sean O'Casey, and in England, by the '60s and '70s, the urge to capture this kind of truth onstage emerged in a new movement called hyperrealism, as exemplified by the plays of David Storey and Arnold Wesker.

At first the naturalist movement was akin to realism, and they shared the same goal: to show onstage, in a scientific manner, how we can solve our problems.

But naturalism soon went a different route. Where the realist movement was shaped by the writings of Auguste Comte and the cause-to-effect worldview of Isaac Newton, the naturalists took their cue from Darwin's *Origin of Species*. In this seminal work, Darwin was emulating the scientific spirit of the age, trying to show how biological diversity can be explained by the cause-to-effect dynamics of natural selection. Yet where the other sciences had revealed to us a world in which human beings could intervene to improve conditions for themselves, Darwin's scientific mechanism of heredity and environment carried more ominous implications. If natural selection takes millions of years, there is very little you or I can do to alter it or even hurry it along.

Although modern genetics has done much to confirm Darwin's notions about heredity, it also seems to hold out a Faustian hope that someday the naturalist vision will be a thing of the past: genetic engineering may overturn all of our assumptions of what we can or cannot be.

8

Absurdism

After World War II, a major new vision of futility swept across Europe, eventually spreading out to shape and influence playwriting in every corner of the globe. It grew up in part because of the way in which vast populations had been lied to and manipulated by the propaganda machines employed by various governments throughout the war. It grew up in part because people could no longer agree on what the lessons of history were, or even on the nature of the earth-shattering events they had just experienced. And it grew up in part because of the threat of global annihilation, which followed on the heels of World War II under the shadow of the U.S. and Russian nuclear arsenals.

In the wake of these profoundly disorienting experiences, an entirely new model for perceiving the world around us was born. Actors, writers, and directors who sought to bring that vision of life to the stage had literally to devise an entirely new set of dramatic principles. A new approach to playwriting, a new approach to acting, and a new approach to directing—all of these had to be created if the powerful truths underlying this new vision were going to be captured in dramatic form.

This vision was nothing less than a disturbing new realization about the futility of human efforts to produce any noticeable effect on the world around us.

Where the naturalists had postulated scientifically that we cannot change the circumstances of our lives, this new generation of dramatists seemed swept away in a tide of helplessness. Where the naturalists had been depressed by the implications of their insights, this new generation was utterly cut adrift in a world that had no use for them. In the words of Albert Camus, they felt as though they existed without meaning or consequence in a universe that took no notice of them. That universe included nature, government, and society. It included all other human beings.

In 1965, dramatic theorist Martin Esslin dubbed this new vision of life theatre of the absurd. It had been brought most irrefutably and shockingly to life by Samuel Beckett, almost fifteen years earlier, in his watershed tragicomedy *Waiting for Godot*. With this play, Beckett altered forever the way playwrights tell stories, construct characters, and write dialogue. The inner truths captured by theatre of the absurd are so powerful and so inescapable, that, to some extent, nearly every dramatic form—whether realist, epic, melodramatic, or comic—has to incorporate some element of absurdism, or it runs the risk of appearing to have completely overlooked what may be the most important insights of our time.

What are those insights?

First, there is the notion that human beings cannot produce change. This is a notion that we have examined in earlier chapters. It is an essential element of every vision of futility. But something new and profoundly disturbing had been added to it after World War II.

Where the naturalists had said, yes, nothing we do will produce change, they had arrived at that conclusion through scientific reasoning. And, they had Darwin to provide an explanation: The futility of our efforts is guaranteed by the unchangeable nature of environment and heredity. Oddly enough, this was in and of itself a comforting realization, because, to the naturalists, the reasons for our ineffectualness could be both known and understood.

The absurdists, however, took their cue from existentialism, not science. And though existentialism seeks to identify the irrational but irrefutable angst of alienation that exists in every one of us, it makes no attempt to provide a logical explanation.

Feeling this terror is simply the price we pay for being alive.

And that terror is not just confined to the recognition that we are unable to produce change. It also grows out of the fact that we cannot communicate, either. We cannot communicate, because nothing in this world has fixed meaning. Words, signs, symbols, gestures, facial expressions only *seem* to have meaning because each of us as an individual, in our existential cocoon, has assigned them meaning. Arbitrary meanings. Meanings that cannot be shared or agreed upon because none of us has any way of knowing what anyone else is actually trying to say.

Esslin tries to illustrate our inability to communicate with each other in the following way: Suppose, he wrote, that person A has fallen in love, and he tries to relate this feeling to a friend, person B. He says, "I am in love." What effect does this word *love* have on person B? Why, B merely remembers what it feels like when he himself is in love. So instead of communicating what he's feeling, A has simply triggered B's feelings, which may be quite different from A's. No communication has occurred.

Often we try to communicate by citing external sources—great poetry, literature, the words of famous people. But none of these has any inherent, fixed meaning. To one person, *The Merchant of Venice* is a profoundly sympathetic rendering of the dilemma of Jews in a Christian nation; to another, it is an attack on those same people. If you try to argue the point, what happens? All too often the "discussion" descends into endless rounds of hairsplitting that usually lead to worse confusion than existed before the discussion commenced.

Any effort to communicate with words will be useless.

Any effort to communicate with gestures will be ridiculous.

Any attempt to cite external sources, pointless.

However, it is one thing to realize the truth of these statements. It is quite another to put them onstage in a way that audiences will find compelling. Philosophizing about the issues will not hold an audience's attention. Every play, every story performed onstage has to be *acted*. The characters must be *doing* something specific. But how is that possible, if you want to demonstrate a vision of a cosmos in which action is not possible and nothing can be communicated?

You, the writer, have to give the actors something to do. And giving the actors something to do means that in some way, their characters have to be pursuing change.

Here is the key to dramatizing the absurdist vision of life: Yes, the characters are pursuing change, but the pursuit always leads them back to exactly where they started.

This was the breakthrough that Beckett made back in the 1950s. Since acting is to take action, give your characters actions that produce no change. Borrowing from medieval theatre, film, and literature, as well as vaudeville, Beckett created a dramatic form in which human activity always travels in a circle.

Thus, early in *Waiting for Godot*, Vladimir tries to make a point about the two thieves who died with Christ on Mount Calvary. Estragon, at first indifferent, eventually begins to pay attention to what Vladimir is telling him, but the closer he listens, the more confused he becomes. He can't quite grasp what Vladimir means by "Saviour"— what precisely did He save us from? Death, or hell? Vladimir is unable to clarify this point, but he presses on desperately with his thesis. Of the four Evangelists, Vladimir says, only two mention that there were thieves present on Mount Calvary, and only one of the two says that one of the thieves was saved. Estragon, meanwhile, has gotten lost in the crosscurrent of numbers. Two of what? Two thieves? Two Evangelists? And one reported that one did what? In the end, all that Estragon can do is declare that the whole thing is a waste of time.

Nothing has been communicated. Nothing has been changed. But the characters were pursuing change nevertheless.

This type of circular dialogue is the central technique of the playwright who wants to capture absurdism on the stage. It can be found in the work of almost every writer whose work is tinged with the vision of futility, from Beckett and Ionesco to Harold Pinter and Tom Stoppard. Even explosive plays charged with dramatic change can be given an added measure of truth by steeping the dialogue with this circular banter. David Mamet is a master of this style, and plays such as his *American Buffalo* and his *Oleanna* are built on the mounting frustrations of characters who can break out of their circular attempt to communicate only with an eruption of violence.

Circular dialogue has its counterpart in circular activity.

Waiting for Godot is full of examples of this. In the opening scene of the play, we meet the two tramps,

Vladimir and Estragon, engaged in what is basically a reasonable activity, yet one that is ultimately pointless. Each of them is being irritated by an item of clothing. Estragon is removing his boot because something inside it is bothering him. Vladimir examines the lining of his hat for the same reason. Neither man finds what he's looking for, no matter how many times he repeats the action. Later on, when Pozzo and Lucky stop by, Lucky is ordered to dance for their amusement. The dance is executed but accomplishes nothing. Then, in Act II, the tramps discover that Lucky has left his hat behind. The two men amuse themselves with the three hats they now possess, donning, doffing, and exchanging them in rapid sequence. Delightfully amusing, but again, pointless. It's circular activity that leaves them no different from when they started.

The incident with the three hats suggests nothing if not the antics of vaudeville comedians. This is another area Beckett borrowed from in his effort to fill his play with behavior that leads nowhere. Vladimir and Estragon try to figure out how to hang themselves. One tramp tries to get the other to pull his trousers up as high as they'll go. And then there's the elaborate business of Lucky trying to carry Pozzo's baggage. All of these owe their inspiration to vaudeville and the comic routines of British music hall performers.

To what end? Why has Beckett included them in his play?

Like all slapstick comedy, it keeps us amused while we come to terms with the fact that nothing is ever going to change.

One significant feature that absurdism shares with the naturalist vision of life is the belief that gradually, over time, things will get worse. Thus, in *Waiting for Godot*, there are two occasions in which the tramps consider hanging themselves, but on the second occasion they actually try to do it. There are two occasions in which Estragon sleeps, but the second time he has a terrible nightmare. Pozzo and Lucky join them twice, but on the second visit, Pozzo has gone blind and Lucky is mute. So, yes, there is change, but it is beyond the control of the characters. It is the change that comes from entropy, decay, despair, and disability.

In Tom Stoppard's *Rosencrantz and Guildenstern Are Dead*, we see all of the principles of absurdist construction employed in the service of an Elizabethan costume drama. The protagonists are unable to have the slightest effect on events around them. They while the time away in tangled wordplay. They make plans but are unable to take action. And they play pointless games. In one such game they try to sustain a conversation in which every response to every question is itself a question. Meanwhile, their anxiety is mounting into existential terror, as they are sent unwittingly to their deaths at the hand of the king of England.

Even realist drama can benefit from the underlying sense of futility that the absurdist vision imparts to a play. *The Gin Game* is a Pulitzer Prize–winning social drama by D. L. Coburn that examines the essential inhumanity of the American custom of warehousing our seniors in old folks homes. Stripped down to its bare essentials—two characters, one setting—Coburn's play seeks to expose the hopelessness and emptiness of life ignored. But he places his drama squarely on a foundation of circular activity: day in and day out, the only thing that brings the gentleman Weller and and his new lady friend, Fonsey, together is Weller's insistence that they play yet another round of gin. Weller's anger mounts throughout the drama because he is unable to win a single hand. Eventually Fonsey plays badly to allow him to win. This enrages Weller even more. In the end, even their pointless, circular activity becomes unbearable. They are unable to play at all. They are left with nothing.

Summary of the Absurdist Vision

The absurdist vision of life expresses the belief that we live in a world to which we have no meaningful relationship. We cannot change anything and we cannot communicate anything. The best we can do is find some way to occupy our time while the inexorable forces of entropy and decay grind us down. In this way, change will ultimately occur: things will get worse. A summary of key absurdist techniques that will bring this vision to the stage follows.

Non–action Structure in an Absurdist Play

Absurdism does not use what can properly be called an action structure. The characters pursue change, but the results are either pathetic or hilarious. They are never successful. Changes that do occur fall completely outside the characters' ability to influence events.

1. The situation in which we discover the characters is bleak and hopeless.

2. In a response to this situation, they will embark on a series of circular activities that always lead them right back to where they started.

3. Some of these activities will be directly inspired by the need to find out why they're in this situation and what can be done about it. This might involve:

   - asking questions of each other
   - reviewing the information available to them
   - attempting to affect or summon other characters who may or may not exist.

4. Characters will pursue some of these activities knowing full well they won't produce change but

are simply intended to kill time. Such activities include the following:

- pointless philosophical arguments
- hairsplitting over the meanings of words or actions
- telling jokes
- playing games.

5. Or the characters might become involved in *preventing* each other from doing these things, by interrupting a bad joke or an often-repeated story or a pointless philosophical discourse. When this line of activity is pursued, however, it, too, often proves ineffectual.

Mastering the use of circular behavior is only one part of successfully bringing the absurdist vision to the stage. A play filled with the kinds of activity described here can easily feel as if it's going nowhere. When that happens, your audience will get bored and restless. There are specific, essential features of absurdism that must be incorporated into your script to avoid this. The qualities listed in the following section are what truly distinguish absurdism as a vision of life and separate it from what might otherwise be just well-written comedy.

6. The use of repeated elements can engage the audience's attention in unexpected and provocative ways.

- A character or a group of characters might arrive and leave on two or more occasions.
- An incident offstage or onstage may occur repeatedly throughout the play.
- A phrase, an unusual word, or an exchange of dialogue might be repeated throughout the play.

7. These repeated elements, however, should never happen exactly the same way twice. Instead, there should be a slight difference each time they occur. This will heighten the extent to which they intrigue and draw the audience in.

   - Something should be different about the characters who reenter.
   - The repeated incident should never occur exactly the same way.
   - The phrasing or the placement of repeated words should vary, or the words should be spoken by different characters.

8. Over time, the conditions surrounding your characters should worsen.

9. Over time, the emotional or psychological distress of your characters should deepen.

10. The events and actions of the play must unfold against a background of alienation and fear. That is the essence of the absurdist message: Our ineffectualness may lead us to do funny and ridiculous things, but it is at core a frightening state of existence that, in the end, kills all hope.

Background to the Development of Absurdism

Theatre of the absurd grew out of a general feeling of despair that swept across Europe after World War II, first documented by a group of intellectuals known as the existentialists. These philosophers, poets, and playwrights were the earliest writers to identify the inner angst and the terrible feeling of helplessness that seemed to be the condition of modern humanity. In their work, they observed that any effort of human beings to achieve a fixed set of moral values, or a way of perceiving the world that we can all agree to—much less a plan for improving the world— was an exercise in futility.

Albert Camus pointed out in 1943, in his essay "The Myth of Sisyphus," that human beings live in an irrational universe that can never be affected by our hopes or plans. Jean Paul Sartre went further. He asserted, as Nietzsche had, that God—or, at least, any effective concept of God—is dead and that heaven is empty. Therefore, there can be no fixed standards of conduct or verifiable moral codes. We live in a world that cannot provide us with useful or effective moral guidance. And yet, traditionally, people have always counted on the values and the structure of their society to help them know who they are, how they should behave, and what they can expect from life.

So, if there are no reliable moral codes or standards of conduct, then what will define us? How will we know what to do? How will we know who we are?

Sartre basically asserted that each of us has to decide for himself or herself who we are and by what standard we will live. And having decided that, we must accept responsibility for the consequences of it.

That is the great torment of being human.

That is the curse of being free: everyone is responsible for everything. Freedom carries with it the anguish of this responsibility.

In the 1930s and '40s, a generation of existential dramatists created a body of theatre to articulate and disseminate these principles. Among them are Camus, Jean Giraudoux, and Jean Anouilh, as well as Sartre. Sartre's *No Exit* is the unrivaled masterpiece of the genre. In their plays and in their philosophical writings, the existentialists argued that, since we have to decide for ourselves what we believe, we should not allow ourselves to be persuaded by what *others* believe.

But this is inherently contradictory. After all, they themselves were using arguments to persuade us not to be persuaded by arguments.

When absurdism appeared in the early 1950s, it was in part a response to the inadequacies of existential theatre. This new group of playwrights set out to simply create a world onstage in which no one can affect anyone, all meaningful communication fails, and nothing changes. In essence, they invented a world in which all of the principles of existentialism apply—including the pointlessness of talking about it.

Along with Samuel Beckett, playwrights like Eugene Ionesco, Jean Genet, and Arthur Adamov experimented with remarkably different approaches to this new vision. In America, Edward Albee and Arthur Kopit brought fresh absurdist inspiration to the theatre, as did Christopher Durang. It is one of the dominant influences in David Mamet's and Sam Shepard's work, and the recent success of work like David Ive's *All in the Timing* continues to prove that this particular vision of futility speaks to audiences in powerful and significant ways.

9

Romanticism

There is a part of us that believes that the human spirit is the most important aspect of our existence and, if we attend to its needs, we will be happy. But another part of us says the opposite: Our physical side is paramount, and it is through physical experiences that we find the greatest joy. It is a deeply contradictory set of beliefs, and it is only one such set of contradictions we carry around inside us.

For example, many of us believe that some things are eternal, whether it's the human soul or great ideas; some things will never perish. And yet, at the same time, we also know that everything comes to an end, a perception recognized in the phrase *nothing lasts forever.*

Yet another example: Many of us often have the feeling that certain experiences or qualities in this world can be unlimited, whether it is pleasurable sensations or family togetherness. But within us, when we reflect coldly on the matter, we know that there can be only a finite amount of any given item or experience.

This stew of contradictions inside us has led numerous philosophers and artists to the recognition that human beings live constantly in a state of turmoil, that we are divided, internally, against ourselves. It is an irrational state of affairs that drives us constantly to seek experiences and qualities we can never have. Recognizing this paradox helped lead to the birth of one of the most seductive and persuasive visions of life: romanticism.

Not romanticism in the sense of Hollywood movies or candlelit dinners, romanticism in the sense that it was originally meant, when it was first identified as one of the most devastating aspects of human existence: the belief that we are doomed to pursue things we can never have.

And the short list of dualities mentioned here is only the tip of the iceberg when it comes to understanding why the human heart is so filled with unrest. Another pivotal set of contradictions we live with is the feeling that every human being must be treated as an individual, each with his or her own individual truth. But at the same time we have an overwhelming sense that there are higher truths, truths that reach beyond our existence on this earth. And this contradiction between personal and universal truth is one of the keys to understanding romanticism. For the romantic believes two things:

- If such a universal truth exists, it can be found only by knowing and experiencing as much of the world as possible.
- But simultaneously, that truth can be found full and undiluted in every individual item on this planet.

The artist or the writer who seeks to discover the great truths about life is encouraged to experience as much of the world as possible. But even the artist who is confined to one room, or to the view of one garden, can understand the full nature of life by studying a single flower.

It's clearly another contradiction. The romantics sought to resolve that conflict by getting as close as possible to those things in this world that are the nearest to their natural state. The more altered something is, the harder it is to find the truth within it. Things and places dominated by human manufacture are the most false.

Consequently, the romantic seeks nature and shuns cities. By living in the country, one gets closer to the truth and becomes a better person. Conversely, people who live in the city tend to be dishonest and too sophisticated to be trusted.

For the romantic, the world is full of good and bad people—with very little in between. Those who are good and noble are usually fighting a losing battle, but they fight on because they can't help themselves. They are by nature good people. They believe in the highest ideals and they can accept nothing less in the world around them.

The people they fight against—who are, if you will, the villains of the world—are men and women who have decided there's nothing wrong with lust, greed, or ambition. These are people who have given themselves over to their lowest appetites. They could hold those appetites in check but refuse to do so.

And the greatest weapon these people use is the power of reason.

Think about it. Whenever we fight for a principle or an ideal, we are constantly informed by those who oppose us that we are being unreasonable. Calmly, logically, they explain that what we're asking for doesn't make sense. We're told to use our heads. But an irrational voice inside tells us that, however much their arguments make sense, this ideal for which we have taken a stand cannot be abandoned. We are right even though we can't justify our actions with fancy logic.

How do we know we are right?

Our hearts tell us so.

And what our hearts tell us, logic can never disprove.

This is the essence of the romantic view of life: Emotions can always be trusted.

Lies, on the other hand, are manufactured by the intellect. The intellect is not to be trusted. No, we must follow our hearts.

When this view of life was first formulated at the end of the eighteenth century, it swept across Europe with unprecedented impact. It led to revolutions in philosophy, religion, and politics. It fueled the violent overthrow of the British government in America and the monarchy in France. And it empowered artists in every discipline to explore astonishing new forms and styles.

These potent new romantic principles, for example, inspired Beethoven, Brahms, Schubert, Tchaikovsky, and Wagner, among others. English poetry saw its most brilliant age come to flower under the heady inspiration of romanticism. Byron, Keats, Shelley, and Tennyson found the source of their immortal work in these ideas. In America, Longfellow and Poe followed suit. And great novels sprang from this inspiration as well, in the work of Alexandre Dumas, Gustave Flaubert, and Victor Hugo.

It was as though the human heart had been unleashed after centuries of imprisonment, and to this day that revolution of the emotions has retained a powerful influence over the way we see the world, the way we respond to the actions of others, and the way we judge those around us.

It became nothing more or less than a new vision of life.

How did playwrights respond to this heady new emotional brew? What new dramatic forms did they create to capture this vision of life onstage?

That is a difficult and disappointing question to answer. Playwrights who aspired to write in the romantic style, and the theorists who guided them, advocated an approach to drama in which no attention at all would be paid to the plot. Instead, the focus was on developing deeply complex characters full of contradictions, creating a moody atmosphere onstage, and then allowing the characters to give vent to their emotions in the most elevated language possible.

And, by our standards today, almost every play written in this manner was a disaster.

Even in the nineteenth century, which was the great age of romanticism, audiences were not much interested in these long-winded, pretentious verse dramas. Simply put, they are unwatchable.

If this seems like a harsh judgment, note that almost no plays written in this era are performed anymore. Even the most noteworthy dramas—Victor Hugo's *Hernani*, Alexander Pushkin's *Boris Godunov*, Friedrich Schiller's *Mary Stuart*, James Sheridan Knowles' *William Tell*—are seldom seen outside college theatre or classic conservatory productions.

It wasn't until late in the nineteenth century, when the romantic movement was almost dead, that a lasting piece of theatre was written that truly brought to the stage the poetic insights of this new aesthetic in a way audiences have enjoyed ever since: *Cyrano de Bergerac* by Edmond Rostand.

And although the characters and situations of *Cyrano* are saturated with the influence of romantic thinking, it's important to note that the structure of the play is not. Modernism had taken hold of the stage by this late date. The importance of a solid, plausible plot had returned to the forefront. And the plot of *Cyrano* is a winner: A brilliant poet and swordsman who loves a lady with the depth and capacity for which we all hunger can never speak of his love because of his plain, unheroic face. He feels as though he would be mocking love itself if, with his large, unattractive nose, he uttered words of deep emotion. Like the true romantic hero, he finds this unacceptable, because he believes in the highest ideals and will not compromise those ideals even the slightest.

But when Cyrano learns that a handsome young cadet named Christian also loves Roxanne, he offers to write poetry for the unlettered soldier to use in wooing her. In this way, Cyrano finally gets to speak of his emotions without disgracing his idealized notion of love. And in this way, he ultimately wins Roxanne's heart.

In the romantic vision of life, however, we are doomed to yearn for things we can never have. And the most devastating of these is love.

Consequently, in *Cyrano de Bergerac*, Christian dies before he has a chance to tell Roxanne that Cyrano wrote the poetry that won her over, that in fact it is Cyrano's mind and heart she really loves. But after Christian dies, Cyrano can never tell Roxanne the truth. How ignoble would it be to say such a thing about a man, especially a man who is dead and can no longer defend himself? Cyrano is prepared to go to his own grave having never revealed what transpired.

But fate has another twist in store for them. On the day that Cyrano succumbs to an assassin's wounds, Roxanne pieces the truth together herself—too late. She has lost twice the only man she ever loved. Cyrano's only consolation is that he dies knowing his ideals were never compromised.

True romanticism might very well be the most heart-wrenching of all the visions of futility.

It is a belief system that puts our emotions at the center of the universe, and it makes love the most important of those emotions. Of all the passions that surge through the human soul, love is the most spiritual and the most inexplicable. We are helpless in its grip. And it cannot be controlled by any use of reason or logic. Indeed, it is so powerful it can inflict death. In the romantic view of life, love is a form of madness.

It's easy to see, then, that for romantics, the world is a place of intoxicating extremes.

And the allure of those extreme ideas is as strong now as it ever was. Although romanticism failed to generate a lasting body of work in drama the way it did in music and literature, it continues to influence playwriting throughout the world, but in a very different way.

Unlike the other visions of life we have examined in this book, the romantic vision is not a structure that must be followed in order to capture a particular notion of how the world works. Rather, romanticism is a set of truths, or ethical principles, that drives the characters to extreme actions and—like the guiding moral code that governs an epic play—determines the outcome of the story for each character.

Romanticism can take any of the forms we have previously discussed. It can appear in realism, in naturalism, or in epic form. But the playwright with a romantic vision will charge that overarching structure with specific qualities dictated by the principles of romanticism. For example, the main character will be struggling to achieve something ideal in the face of overwhelming odds. He or she will be guided by his or her heart to work toward a goal that seems irrational and unachievable. The blocking characters will try to reason with the hero, explaining why the only sensible thing to do is to abandon this goal. And in its bleakest form, the romantic hero will finally be crushed by life's realities.

The plays of Tennessee Williams are examples of powerful modern work that is saturated with the influence of romanticism, even while it is utilizing some of the other styles we've touched on already. In *The Glass Menagerie*, Tom Wingfield is driven by a hunger to be free from his mother. It is one of those overwhelming, irrational, yet inescapable passions so characteristic of the romantic hero. Specifically, he wants to travel the world, to see and experience as much as he can, seeking truth in the way that every romantic yearns to. The only thing holding him back is concern for his emotionally dependent, slightly crippled sister, Laura. The mother, Amanda, who is a character constructed with tremendous psychological complexity and is as much a victim of her own romantic yearnings as Tom is, nevertheless attempts to solve their dilemma rationally. And that very rationality is what spells disaster for them. At Amanda's prompting, Tom invites a young man from work to meet his sister. Unintentionally, the young man breaks Laura's heart, and in the emotional explosion that follows, Tom leaves his family once and for all. True to the romantic vision of life— the belief that we can never have the things we most desperately seek—Tom gets his life of adventure, but it is empty for him now. He is haunted till the end of his days by the memory of his heartbroken sister and his abandoned mother.

Notice that, as true as it is to the romantic vision, *The Glass Menagerie* has little to do with romantic love. Love does loom huge in the romantic world, but it is not the only thing we seek. Any passionately embraced ideal or goal will suffice. In Paul Zindel's *Effect of Gamma Rays on Man-in-the-Moon Marigolds*, the romantic hero is an elementary school girl, Tillie, who hungers for the poetry of science. Her mother is the blocking character who tells Tillie to stop daydreaming and see the world as it really is. Against all odds—including poverty, an antagonistic older sister, and a devastating home life—Tillie wins the school science fair. But in the end she is humiliated by her mother's drunken misconduct and the cold-blooded slaughter of the pet rabbit that provided her only source of affection. Less bleak than *The Glass Menagerie*, however, this play leaves us with the knowledge that Tillie will rise above these cruel events. The pursuit of her passionate ideals is undimmed.

Again, a marvelously romantic drama that has nothing to do with romance.

And when the romantic vision *is* brought to bear on a love story proper, it can raise the stakes and truly pit the lovers against the world. *Burn This* by Lanford Wilson throws together two people who couldn't be more opposite. Anna is a New York City aesthete, a young dancer leading the life of the artiste in Greenwich Village. Pale is a bigoted, insensitive, self-centered loudmouth who derides New York, art, and culture of any kind. Yet both of them are lost souls raw with grief over the death of Pale's homosexual brother. It is in their passion for life, and in their pain, that they are drawn together. And yet the idea that they can ever find happiness as lovers is ridiculous, unreasonable, and irrational; if you will, it is insane. In other words: romanticism in full force.

Summary of the Romantic Vision

As I mentioned earlier, romanticism, unlike the other models we've discussed, is not a structure. Rather, it is a value system and a set of assumptions about the world that place the characters in extreme situations, all the while motivating them to strive for things they can never have. In the following summary, therefore, I have deviated from the approach that has served us so far. Rather than a list of structural guidelines that bring this particular vision to life—for it can actually appear within any structure—here you'll find summarized the key principles that define the world of the romantic and drive the characters forward.

1. The world of the romantic is one of dire extremes. Either the hero is pursuing something against staggering odds, or the couple who yearn to be together come from such different worlds that any hope of success defies reason.

2. The hero is passionate, driven by extreme feelings that he or she cannot effectively put into words.

3. The hero believes in absolute ideals and cannot compromise on any of them.

4. This causes great personal anguish, but the hero cannot help him- or herself. The hero is driven to seek these things by his or her inner nature, something that cannot be changed or reasoned with.

5. The hero is opposed by characters who are swept up in the worst human weaknesses. Often these weaknesses take the form of our lowest appetites—greed, ambition, lust—but they can also be psychological weaknesses, such as vanity, despair, and self-loathing.

6. The villains either openly revel in indulging their appetites or wallow in their weaknesses.

7. In the romantic world, good people lead simple lives. Either they are close to nature or they live in poverty.

8. Villains in the romantic world are often wealthy and lead lives of sophisticated decadence.

9. In the most extreme stories, romantic heroes will risk everything, defying all reason and logic, in order to achieve that which is clearly impossible. They scorn death and failure.

10. The romantic world is a place where all emotions are important, but love has the greatest power of all. It is the one thing most worth striving for. It cancels out every other claim on the hero. It is a form of insanity.

Background on the Development of Romanticism

For most of European history, art has been dominated by the notion that artists should follow rigorous rules learned from their teachers and practiced in a methodical way. It is a notion that can probably be traced to the ancient Greeks, who, for all their passionate love of life, also celebrated the power of the intellect and believed that most good things spring from the mind, not the emotions.

When the Renaissance began in the fourteenth and fifteenth centuries, this classical approach to art was embraced with unbridled enthusiasm throughout the continent. Working from bits and pieces of Aristotle, Plato, and Horace that had survived the Dark Ages, scholars began to assemble increasingly complex and demanding sets of rules that defined what art was and how it should be created. Some countries went so far as to establish official academies that reviewed the work of artists and handed down judgments on whether or not the rules had been properly adhered to.

At the end of the eighteenth century, however, the publication of a single, sensational short story by Johann Wolfgang von Goethe brought centuries of classical tyranny to an end. That story was *The Sorrows of Young Werther*. It tells of a young man who is so devastated by an unrequited love that he kills himself. It was a tremendous success, read everywhere in Europe. Suddenly people began to realize that art could be based on intense emotional experiences and not on a cold, rational set of rules. And it was in Germany that a young group of writers set out to apply that new insight to drama.

They called themselves the Sturm und Drang school of playwrights. In English: Storm and Stress. Their goal was to smash all of the old rules of classical art and establish a whole new approach to theatre. Three key principles they advocated in their work survived and carried over into full-blown romanticism:

- They believed that the rights of individual human beings are sacred and should never be compromised for any reason.
- They dramatized and celebrated the lives of people who were dominated by qualities—passion, egoism, severe mood shifts—that prevented them from ever fitting into society.
- They made heroes out of people who became leaders not because of their ideas—remember, the intellect can never be trusted—but because of the sheer magnetism of their personalities.

Sturm und Drang finally blossomed into romanticism when a group of intellectuals in Berlin founded a journal called *Das Athenaeum*, in which the principles of the writers were expanded upon. It was in *Das Athenaeum* that the term *romanticism* was coined to describe this new revolution in art. When the philosopher August Wilhelm Schlegel took up the cause and codified romanticism, it came to be recognized as a serious body of thought that derived its legitimacy from the teachings of Immanuel Kant. It was Schlegel who most passionately argued that romantics should not worry about the plots of their plays, but instead should focus on characterization, mood, and emotion.

This single piece of advice might alone have been responsible for the flood of unwatchable dramas that were subsequently written.

Although men of letters such as Goethe, Schiller, Lenz, and Shelley composed some remarkable dramatic literature in the thrall of romanticism, in the end it proved to be unsuccessful as a guide for playwrights.

But romanticism did succeed in this regard: It drew to our attention once and for all the soaring idealism that can charge the human soul with passion. It reminded us that there is a greater, more spiritual truth that transcends the mundane inadequacies of this life.

Romanticism never set out to describe the world as it actually exists. It set out to describe the unquenchable, irrational desire we have inside us to fight for ideals even if they are impossible to achieve.

10

Afternote

A Few Words from Naturalism, Absurdism, and Romanticism

Naturalism

As we discussed in Chapter 6, the words *naturalism* and *naturalistic*, in everyday conversation, are often used interchangeably with *realism* and *realistic*. But in dramatic art this would be a mistake. *Naturalism* refers to a style of theatre that tries to put as much of the world as possible, with all its messy details, onstage. Realism strips away the details and leaves only the bare essentials.

One source of potential confusion is that, in literary criticism—as opposed to dramatic criticism—naturalism and realism *do* mean the same thing. Prose fiction and poetry are very different art forms from playwriting, however. Those who do both might want to note this area of overlap.

It is interesting to observe that, by the middle of the twentieth century, *naturalism* had fallen out of vogue as a term of art. When a group of British playwrights led by David Storey attempted to revive the principles of this style in the '60s and '70s, they coined a new word, *hyperrealism*, to describe their efforts. This was due in part to the sense that *naturalism* was an old-fashioned word, which might have made their work seem less innovative.

Of course, the word itself is not important, so long as the underlying concepts are understood. The danger is that using the word imprecisely will blur the playwright's grasp of the ideas.

Absurdism

The word *absurdism* also has important connotations that we can lose sight of. In 1965, Martin Esslin borrowed this word from Albert Camus in order to describe the radical new form of theatre created by Samuel Beckett and Eugene Ionesco. But he understood fully what Camus had intended to signify with it.

In his essay, "The Myth of Sisyphus," Camus describes the ineffectualness of our efforts to act or communicate. He called this having an *absurd* relationship to the universe. In this context, absurd doesn't mean ridiculous or funny. It means "out of harmony," that is to say, alone and without meaning or relevance in the world.

It is important to distinguish between this use of the word and the commonplace meaning of it, that is, funny or ridiculous.

Scenes written in the absurdist style often are quite funny, but the humor is of secondary importance. What defines the absurdist world is the underlying fear and anxiety of the characters—an existential terror that grows out of their meaningless isolation from the universe and from each other.

In some ways, fear and anxiety operate in an absurdist play the same way environment operates in a naturalist play. In an absurdist play, fear and anxiety *are* the environment, and they saturate the characters as well as the whole scene.

Romanticism

When the editors of *Das Athenaeum* conceived the word *romanticism* to describe the new movement in art that was catching fire all around them, they wanted to achieve certain things with it.

First off, they chose a word that contained within it an inescapable reminder of the fact that classical art had not always ruled Europe. After the fall of Rome in 476 A.D., the classical order more or less vanished from the continent, preserved only in the eastern European realm known as the Byzantine Empire. Western Europeans were left to reinvent art from scratch, and they did.

In the Middle Ages, a whole new approach to architecture, painting, literature, and drama was developed. Medieval Europeans themselves coined the word *Romanesque* to describe their efforts.

But in the use of this word, we run into the first of a series of amusing coincidences. Medieval architects, inspired by the ruins of Roman buildings around them, were actually trying to create new structures that were Roman-like. This is what Romanesque means, although it eventually came to be applied to other types of art as well. Specifically, the writers of prose fiction, who were concocting elaborate, multiplot stories that spanned many years and locales, were imitating the work of Ovid, and they, too, called their work Romanesque. These "romance" novellas were a great source of inspiration for Shakespeare, who borrowed the plots for many of his plays from them. In doing so, he violated nearly every rule of classical art that existed. Yet he still managed to create some of the greatest drama ever written.

Jump ahead to the eighteenth century.

The editors of *Das Athenaeum* and their compatriots, eager to destroy the rules of classical art once and for all, needed a great playwright to serve as a model for their own work, as well as a vindication of their radical new ideas. And it was Shakespeare who fit the bill. Since the Bard of Avon had been inspired by the Romanesque stories of the Middle Ages, they took the root word, *Roman*, and so came to describe themselves as romantics.

There is a final irony in all of this.

The Romans, of course, admired and imitated Greek art—classical art—in almost every aesthetic endeavor of their own. However, they added an interesting, peculiarly Roman flourish to it. Unlike the Greeks, they didn't believe that good things come only from the intellect. They were comfortable with the idea that extreme experiences can also be an important way to learn about who we are and what the gods expect of us. Roman poets wrote about the delights of extreme emotions, Roman dramatists staged plays full of excessive violence, and, of course, Roman orgies and gladiator contests manifested the same impulse.

The romantics of the eighteenth and nineteenth centuries did not imagine the Romans were the model for their new style of art, yet by an accident of linguistics, they chose a word to describe themselves that means exactly what they intended: in the romantic vision of life, extreme experiences, emotions, and actions are indispensable if you wish to know the truth. As the poet William Blake, a champion of the principles of romanticism, wrote: it is the road of excess that leads to the palace of wisdom.

11

Expressionism

There is a great deal of logic underlying both the vision of change and the vision of futility. Those who feel that change is possible in this world can support their position by explaining the dynamics of cause-to-effect sequences. And those who feel that no change is possible have logic on their side as well; the naturalists are the most scientific of this group, but there is an underlying logic to the arguments of the absurdists and the romantics as well.

For many of us, however, the whole notion of logic misses the point. Too much of what happens in life simply can't be reduced to arguments and rational constructs. There is at the core of life an inexplicable force that speaks to our mystical side in a way that eludes all efforts of the human mind to make sense of it. The reasonable or well-argued drama that dominates most of the theatre seems empty or shallow to those of us who feel this way.

For us, the most truthful kind of theatre is enshrouded in what can only be called a vision of mystery. It is a way of looking at the world that began to take hold of European artists during that time when rationalism in all its many forms was losing its grip on our imaginations and was being rejected by artists, thinkers, and ordinary people everywhere. It emerged on the stage exactly when realism and naturalism—those most scientific of worldviews—were at the peak of their power.

It was as though playwrights—and audiences—felt profoundly unsatisfied by the notion that life could be explained in the mundane language and situations of realistic drama. And one of the great inspirations for breaking away from the logical, realistic worlds that were dominating the European stage at this time was the growing exposure Western artists and writers were getting to Asian theatre.

Asian theatre does not try to re-create objective reality on the stage. It uses color, dance, song, and movement to exaggerate the world and show it symbolically or through a series of highly stylized conventions. And at the end of the nineteenth century, European theatre artists were more open to these ideas than ever before. They yearned for more dynamic and colorful ways of expressing themselves. They wanted a theatre filled with flourishes of movement, explosions of color, music, and a more sensational use of the human voice. In short, they wanted a way to capture the inner mystery of life onstage, something that dramatizing objective reality could never accomplish. The bright, shocking, and poetic dramas of Japan and China in many ways set them free to do this. Later, the puppet theatre of Korea and the dance theatre of Bali added fuel to the fire.

In an effort to bring these colorful flourishes of the human spirit to European drama, a group of writers created a body of revolutionary new plays. Those plays gave birth to the two visions of mystery we will examine here, expressionism and surrealism. These two dramatic styles were conceived almost simultaneously, but it was expressionism that first reached its most fully developed state.

Expressionism is a vision of life that tells us this: The most important truths are not evident in the physical world that is observed and recorded by our senses. The most important truths are contained in the irrational, inexplicable realm of the human psyche. It is the human psyche that provides the driving force for everything significant we do—our fears, our nightmares, our hopes, our yearnings, our terror. If change happens, it is because of them. If change is canceled out or paralyzed, likewise, it is because of them.

The expressionist believes that both human tragedy and human triumph spring from these ungovernable, illogical forces. In 1917, the German writer Ludwig Rubiner tried to share some insight into how this works in his brilliant essay "Der mensch in der mitte." Like much of German thought, it is difficult to translate accurately into English. In essence, the title means "humanity at the center of all things," although "the person in the middle" would be a closer word-for-word translation. In his essay, Rubiner states categorically that the new generation of artists has no patience for slow work. They do not believe in slow work. They believe in *intensity*—in the unlimited passion of giving yourself over completely and illogically to the ideas surging through your heart and mind—and that this intensity will produce change in a way that is tantamount to a miracle. Because when we free ourselves to pursue the sheer joy of the human experience, the intensity of our joy will destroy the prison of commonplace, everyday life in which we presently live.

"If you are a true artist," he declared, "you do not write about factories, or radio stations, or automobiles. You write about the lines of force emitted by them—lines of force intersecting and interweaving in space."

And here is the first key to putting the expressionist vision onstage: The expressionist would never write about factories and cars, like a naturalist or a realist. The expressionist understands that what's important is the impact these things have on our psyches, that in our inner minds, we experience them as forces of energy—devastating, searing, excruciating, and sublime. Therefore, you must find a way to put on stage these lines of energy, these forces of the psyche.

You have a range of techniques that will enable you to do this. Outrageous scenery and props can be designed to embody these forces. Lighting and sound effects can be created to lend the proper air of mystery and irrationality to the proceedings. And the characters in your play can be made into startling embodiments of these forces, in the shocking words they speak, in the exaggerated costumes they wear, in their grotesque makeup. Remember that the expressionist playwright makes absolutely no attempt to show the world in a way that resembles objective reality. Instead, he or she attempts to give physical form to the world that exists inside our minds and our emotions.

Expressionism does not re-create the landscape outside of us; it re-creates the landscape *inside* us. The expressionist vision of life frees the writer to put anything onstage, or in the mouths of the characters, that suits this purpose.

The first full-blown expressionist play was *Murderer, the Hope of Women,* by the German painter Oskar Kokoschka. Written in 1901, it remains a startling drama full of searing truths about the devastating impact men and women have on each other and will always have on each other, for all time.

And in the very subject matter of the play, we can see another significant hallmark of the expressionist vision: Expressionists never concern themselves with small issues. They do not write plays about the tenderness of first love or defying your parents. Instead, they write plays about the inhumanity of governments, the corruption of religion, the bleakness of modern life, or, in the case of Kokoschka's play, the irreconcilability of all men and women everywhere.

In *Murderer, the Hope of Women*, we witness the violent, highly stylized, emotionally draining, and intensely sexual encounter between a Man and a Woman inexplicably drawn to each other. He is dressed as a knight in blue armor; she is a lady in red clothes with long yellow hair. A crowd of friends and followers surrounds each of them as they meet for the first time in front of a silhouetted tower.

The Man and the Woman each feel the magnetism of the other, and at first, each tries to break away from the other's thrall. The Woman cries out to her friends, "Who is that stranger, who has cast a spell on me with his eyes?" as the Man stares at her, entranced, asking his companions, "Who is that creature? Like some proud animal, she grazes amidst her friends."

The Man orders his companions to seize her and imprint her flesh with his branding iron. They do so. The Woman breaks free, produces a knife, and cuts a huge gash in the Man's side. Then she locks him in the tower. But she still hungers for him. She sticks her hand through the bars of his cage and jabs at his open wound, but finally she must cry out, "I caught and caged you, yet your love imprisons me." In the final moments of the play, he breaks free and kills everyone who remains on the stage.

The play is an assault on the senses, with a total running time of about fifteen or twenty minutes. What is Kokoschka trying to say in this explosion of color and sound? To some extent, we can only speculate—which, of course, is the mark of all great drama—but there are very strong clues to help us. Every aspect of the encounter between the Man and the Woman, for example, has its analog in real-life encounters between men and women. The Woman being aware of the Man's gaze on her; the Man noticing how she stands out from the others, inquiring among his companions who she is. Then there's a brief section in which the followers of the Man and the Woman confer with each other, each group bragging about how wonderful its leader is. The Man, in what may be a typical gesture of male possessiveness, wants the Woman to belong to him. In Kokoschka's vision, this takes the form of a nightmare, and the Man literally has her branded onstage.

Here is another important key to the expressionist vision: exaggerating the events of this world to the point where they take on nightmarish dimensions. And in a similarly nightmarish move, the Woman gives the Man a deadly counterblow with a knife.

Kokoschka may very well be saying, "How often in our efforts to take possession of the man or woman we love do we only succeed in causing pain? And having hurt him or her, why is it we continue to stab at the emotional wound we've inflicted?" In Kokoschka's play, all of this transpires in extreme actions and images, which are the language of the tormented psyche, because it is in the psyche where wounds are felt most deeply.

Although expressionism is a difficult aesthetic to summarize or define, nevertheless, we can get a sense of the essence of the expressionist style. Stated most simply, expressionism is the physicalization of the forces of the psyche through grotesque distortion of everyday reality.

When undertaken in its most raw, intense form, as with Kokoschka, expressionism is shocking and painful to endure. Therefore, it is almost always short. It is simply too great an assault on the audience's senses to be sustained for much more than fifteen or twenty minutes.

This presents a problem for expressionists who want to take their time and explore their themes in a more complex manner. Longer-running plays have to be less intense. But they also have to have some kind of structure that the audience can make sense of, a structure that makes them feel as though the scenes and events are building to a significant insight or revelation.

There are several ways of accomplishing this. For example, a longer-running expressionist play might be organized around a predictable, unfolding process, such as going on a journey. Many early expressionists constructed their plays so that this journey alluded to the Stations of the Cross, Christ's symbolic journey into Jerusalem and up Mount Calvary to be crucified. Ernst Toller's *Transfiguration* captures just such a journey, from home, to war, to exile, and finally to a state of transcendent wisdom. Georg Kaiser, in *From Morn Til Midnight*, sends his hapless protagonist on a journey through seven scenes, each of which is a day of the week, a cardinal sin, and a sacrament of the Roman Catholic Church.

Another structure for longer-running plays that can capture the expressionist vision is one that imitates or ridicules the structure of Greek drama. This is what I call a mock classical structure, and it contains all the trappings of ancient tragedy. There is a chorus that introduces the play and sings or recites—often badly—between scenes. The scenes are complete mini-dramas between two or three characters, performed on a bare stage or a single set without elaborate scenery changes. Max Frisch uses this mock classical structure for his *Biedermann and the Firebugs*, a scathing attack on middle-class culture in which an entire city searches for two arsonists while the fire department sings idiotic songs after each scene. *The Tooth of Crime* by Sam Shepard strives for a more serious tone, but it is no less expressionistic and no less dependent on the simple structure of Greek tragedy. Here, a rock band serves as the chorus while the hero, Agamemnon-like, is brought low by his rival and nemesis.

Many playwrights who want to capture the expressionist vision onstage often use a basic episodic structure built around the decline and fall of an ordinary person. It is essentially the story of Joseph K. from Franz Kafka's novel *The Trial*, and it seems to capture a sort of archetypal truth about the fears and anxieties of the modern world in a way few other narratives do.

In this structure, the protagonist is an antihero. That is to say, he or she is an ordinary person who lacks heroic qualities and falls prey to all the weaknesses that beset the average Joe—cowardice, lust, selfishness, lack of insight or generosity toward others. In the first scene, we usually meet this antihero in a difficult situation that is becoming increasingly intolerable. The situation is caused by whatever it is the playwright's critiquing—capitalism, war, society's rules, religion, and so on.

Then there is a series of scenes in which the problem is intensified by setbacks that come from out of left field, events or plot twists that no one really causes, but which spring from the underlying condition. In these scenes the usual structure is this: The bulk of the scene is devoted to a quasi-poetic evocation of the playwright's theme. Sometimes this will be a colorful monologue, or it might be a highly theatrical interlude with dance, masks, or outrageous pieces of scenery. Then, at the end of the scene, there will be a sudden, unexpected development that dramatically worsens the situation for the protagonist. This process of worsening continues until the play builds to one of the following endings:

- an ironic twist
- a cataclysmic upheaval
- the death of the protagonist
- the open-ended suggestion that life will just go on.

This structure may be fused with a journey or with a mock classical organization of the scenes. It is the story of Biedermann's decline and fall in Max Frisch's play, for example. Georg Kaiser's protagonist, named only "Cashier," also follows this model.

The great American playwright Elmer Rice gives us a terrific rendering of this story in his expressionist master-piece *The Adding Machine*. Here we meet the hapless Mr. Zero, an accounting clerk who hates his life but anticipates that after twenty years on the job he is going to get promoted. Instead, he gets fired. His browbeating wife, meanwhile, is waiting for him at home, where a dinner party with their mindless friends has begun without him. Mr. Zero arrives and tries to join in the conversation. Within moments, the police come to arrest him. It turns out Mr. Zero has murdered his boss.

Now Mr. Zero is placed on trial, where he tries to explain the circumstances of his life—to no avail. He is sentenced to death and executed. He awakes in the afterlife, where he discovers that heaven is populated with people he doesn't like—criminals, poets, and artists. He can find contentment here only when he is assigned to a mindless accounting job in some remote office of heaven's adminis-tration. And eventually, even that is taken away from him, because after twenty-five years, he is required to go back to Earth and do it all over again.

Summary of the Expressionist Vision

The expressionist vision of life is based on the belief that the driving forces in our world cannot be explained or under-stood by traditional logic. In expressionism, we attempt to come to terms with, and put to use, the great ideas that erupt within the human soul by dramatizing intense, explosive, irrational activity. This type of activity is the only thing that will produce change in the world. And when change fails to occur, it is because of the same incomprehensible forces deep within our psyches. A summary of key expressionist techniques that will bring this vision to the stage follows.

Non-action Structure in an Expressionist Play

The expressionist vision can capture a persuasive rendering of a world in which change occurs or one in which change does not occur. When change does occur, it sometimes springs from actions undertaken by the protagonist or another character. When this is the case, a kind of intuitive action structure falls into place, intuitive because the changes do not grow out of a logical cause-to-effect sequence that can be easily explained. Rather, the change becomes plausible because somehow, mysteriously, it seems to make sense.

For example, when Mr. Zero ends up in heaven—along with all other criminals and artists—it has a kind of intuitive logic to it, so we accept it as a plausible outcome of his actions (murdering his boss). It is this internal, antirational, intuitive truth that expressionism seeks to capture onstage.

1. There are often no reversals. The story begins in a certain direction and continues in that direction until the end.

2. Usually, this is a process of things getting worse for the protagonist.

3. When changes do occur, they are often caused by events that the character has not triggered and has no control over.

4. Some changes, however, can be caused by the protagonist or by other characters.

5. When these types of changes occur, they cannot be explained by ordinary, everyday logic. There is something intuitive, or mysterious, about our willingness to believe that these changes are possible.

Showing a world driven by mysterious causes and effects is central to the expressionist vision of life, which is why I have labeled it a vision of mystery. Plays that have only a hint of this sensibility about them will be characterized by the approach to change outlined here. However, full-blown expressionism goes much further. It brings an explosive, colorful world of irrational forces to the stage, using many of the techniques that follow.

6. Instead of imitating external reality, expressionism gives physical form to the forces of the psyche, using the most extreme language and stagecraft, as well as grotesque distortion of things and people from everyday life.

7. Often, realistic dialogue is thrown out in favor of more explosive, poetic, or evocative speech. Consequently, characters often speak past each other, not to each other.

8. The events of the play are connected by the association of the ideas at work in the play, not by cause-to-effect structure.

9. The play is driven by its theme, not by a plot. Plots tend to be disjointed and often cease to be recognizable as the play progresses. And the themes are always large, earth-shattering issues.

10. The structure of the play will exploit elements of familiar processes, conventional drama, and/or classical drama.

Background to the Development of Expressionism

Expressionism appeared as a new approach to art at the same time life in the industrialized nations of Europe was becoming increasingly fragmented and dislocated. The rise of the industrial revolution meant that more and more people were being relocated from farms into squalid urban environments, where they were faced with a life of unprecedented insecurity. There was no job security. Families did not work together during the day, and parents often saw their children only when they were asleep. Neighbors constantly changed. Disease was rampant. Physical disability from work-related injuries was commonplace even among children.

Therefore, it is not surprising that older, traditional forms of smooth, continuous storytelling began to feel false to modern audiences.

The traditional moral order was also a victim of the upheaval that began with the Industrial Revolution and which intensified as the twentieth century rolled around. Although melodrama tried to reassure us that good people were always rewarded, the evidence to the contrary was simply too overwhelming. Exploitative, hard-hearted capitalists continually reaped the rewards of this life. Honest, hardworking men and women were left out in the cold.

This perception was intensified by the outbreak of World War I.

In this war, the capacity of new technology to hurl sheer quantities of metal through the air had far outstripped our capacity to stop them. And it was the bodies of young recruits that were used for that purpose. The number of innocent young men sent to their deaths—or who were maimed, psychologically scarred, or disabled for life—was simply unprecedented in human experience. Wholesale slaughter was common at places like Verdun, where the Germans dropped one thousand artillery shells onto every square yard of ground, and a million men died in ten months of fighting. And the Battle of the Somme eclipsed Verdun. There, more than one and a third million men died. The shock to England alone, whose brand-new Citizen Army suffered nearly half a million casualties, cannot be overstated.

This devastating moral and physical dislocation found a powerful voice in expressionism. It crystallized first as a movement in painting but quickly spread to the other arts. Drama, fiction writing, and early filmmaking all were inspired by the expressionist vision of life.

If nothing else, expressionism gave voice to the intense disillusionment with science and modern progress that engulfed those who were devastated by the traumas of World War I. If the carnage at Verdun was the fruit of science, then science can no longer be trusted. The rational process of traditional logic can no longer be trusted. Instead, we must unleash the passion and the intensity of the inner human being. Only in this way can we create a peaceful, harmonious society.

Despite the horrors of the Great War, the first generation of expressionists continued to believe that humans are essentially good and that if we are liberated from corrupting institutions imposed on us by the rich and the powerful—religion, the military, and capitalism being foremost among these—we will be able to give ourselves over to our better natures.

Much of that optimism has since gone out of the expressionist vision of life, however, and the bleak downward spiral of Joseph K. has become all too representative of how we feel now.

For even though their belief in humanity survived World War I, the next global war robbed the expressionists of even that.

12

Surrealism

For all their differences, the expressionists have much in common with the realists and the naturalists. Although the expressionist does not trust the scientific methods advocated by realism and naturalism, nevertheless all three groups have a deep-seated need to examine and critique the institutions and ideas that create human misery. As we have seen, realists and naturalists want a logical explanation for why those institutions have gone wrong. The expressionists simply want to destroy them with sheer, unbridled human intensity.

But to many people, the true secret of life, and the deepest level of human experience, is not caught up in such mundane matters. To them, life should not revolve around solving problems or changing society. The heart of life is a shadowy, disturbing, and wonder-filled enigma that can only be experienced and never explained. While other artists struggled to come to terms with reality in a way that would alter or explain conditions on this earth, this new group sought to capture in art a higher or more transcendent reality, so they called themselves sur—or higher—realists.

Like the expressionists, the surrealists sought to challenge the humdrum replication of everyday life that preoccupied realistic drama. They also wanted to break away from the obsession with human psychology that drove so much of what was being done in the theatre then as well as now. Sociology and psychology can describe outer behaviors, but they can never capture the heart of mystery that makes life extraordinary.

In order to bring the experience of that mystery to the stage, playwrights who saw life through surrealist eyes hunted for techniques that would allow them to probe deep beneath the surface of everyday veneers. The primary tool they developed for uncovering the mysterious heart of life was the use of provocative imagery.

By assembling images in tantalizing juxtaposition with one another, the surrealist creates a disturbing and difficult to define sense of forces at work below the surface of the ordinary world. These images are often commonplace objects, events, or words which, when experienced in an ordinary context, seem quite normal. But when juxtaposed with each other in a startling and unexpected context, the objects, events, or words become charged with unsettling and elusive meanings.

Thus the surrealist avoids *telling* us life is special, or provocative, or mysterious. Instead, he or she will create a situation in which we actually *experience* life's mystery, inexplicably summoned up from the depths of our unconscious perceptions. In this way, the vision of life the writer wants to communicate is contained within the structure of the play itself.

Maurice Maeterlinck was one of the first playwrights to experiment with these nonrational, nonverbal techniques for summoning enigma to the stage. His atmospheric, disturbing play *The Blind* takes place on an island, where an ancient forest overlooks the crashing sea below. There is a hospice that cares for the blind on this island, and every day an old priest leads a group of patients out to a meadow where they can get some fresh air. As the play opens, we discover these twelve men and women in the dark, moonlit night, wondering why their caretaker has not returned to lead them back to the hospice.

In fact, the priest is dead.

He sits at the rear of the stage, his back against an ancient tree, exactly as he was when he passed away earlier in the day.

This is Maeterlinck's first image.

Twelve lost souls, helpless and blind, counting on a holy man to return and lead them safely home, unaware that the man for whom they are waiting is dead and sits in their midst. And all around them, a dark forest looms with increasing menace.

There are several ways to appreciate the impact of this opening scene on an audience. We can impose a traditional literary analysis, for example, and note that the situation is a metaphor for modern life, the way we have been abandoned by our leaders and the way we lack real information about what is happening in the world—our blindness, as it were.

Or, we can be tantalized by the religious symbolism Maeterlinck is playing with. Are the twelve blind men and women a symbol for the twelve apostles? Then who does the thirteenth figure, the dead priest, symbolize? Judas was the thirteenth apostle, and he betrayed the others, so is the dead priest a symbol for Judas? Or perhaps he is Christ, the holy man who leads us. In that case, perhaps Maeterlinck is saying that it was really Christ who betrayed us when he died and left us here alone.

This kind of intellectual analysis can be useful in helping define the parameters of possible meanings the playwright is trying to invoke, but it's important to remember that absolutely none of these interpretations is hinted at in the text, either in the stage directions or in what the characters say to one another. Maeterlinck is not interested in obvious metaphors, and the power of the play transcends mere intellectual games.

In *Waiting for Godot*, Samuel Beckett plays with a lot of the same material. Religious images frame the absence of an all-important personage. In this case it's Godot, who never appears to assist our hapless heroes. Beckett was asked over and over in his lifetime who Godot symbolized, specifically, is Godot really God, for whose return we wait in vain? In every case, Beckett replied that, if he knew who Godot was, he'd have said so in the script. He wrote his play precisely because none of us knows for whom, or for what, we are waiting.

To some extent, we must extend the same lesson in retrospect to Maeterlinck. Perhaps Maeterlinck had a particular meaning in mind when he sat down to write the play, but the potency of the images he created transcends that meaning.

And so we arrive at a whole other way of understanding the power that can be tapped into with surrealist construction: savoring its pure visual impact. As we read the play we must see the stage, the costumes, and the characters and appreciate with our inner eyes the way in which they provoke our unconscious minds into conscious agitation, like tremors on the ocean's floor.

At the start of *Old Times*, Harold Pinter also experiments with surrealist imagery. A married couple is talking about a houseguest who is going to arrive soon and spend the night with them. The houseguest, Anna, is an old chum of the wife, but neither woman has seen the other for more than a decade. So the husband and the wife speculate about the absent Anna.

But provocatively, Pinter has placed Anna right in the room, standing silently while she is being discussed, unseen by the others, though clearly visible to us. It is a simple trick, but it lends layers of resonance to the scene, resonance that simply cannot be captured or explained in words.

In an earlier play, *The Dumbwaiter*, Pinter uses surrealist events and objects to create an air of menace, as two Cockney thugs wait in an abandoned hotel for the arrival of the man they must kill. Inexplicably, an old dumbwaiter in the room comes to life, delivering ordinary objects that somehow now are charged with mystery. And in the final moment of the play, one of them turns out to be, in fact, the designated victim, through an eerie yet physically impossible surprise entrance.

In *Ashes to Ashes*, Pinter demonstrates his superb command of a very different surrealist technique. Here, the provocative images are not physically present in the objects or characters that appear onstage. They are imbedded in the words the characters speak.

Ashes to Ashes presents us with another couple discussing an absent character. Like *Old Times*, the play opens midconversation. And it opens with an image. But the image is contained in the words the wife, Rebecca, speaks to her husband. Everything else about the setting and the characters is quite ordinary. Still, within moments, a powerful spell has been cast on us, as Rebecca tells of an encounter with a former lover of hers.

The image she describes is one of the lover presenting his fist to her, drawing her head toward it with his free hand, and telling her to kiss it. This is followed by another image. Rebecca would ask her lover to place his hands on her throat, which he did, pushing her backward until her legs parted.

The picture conjured up in our minds by Pinter's words is disturbing—and inexplicable. There are significant themes implied in these images—domination, violence, sexuality—but it's equally clear that this was a voluntary relationship and it seems that no physical harm was done to either party.

As the husband, Devlin, continues to question his wife about this ex-lover, Pinter's surrealist strategy continues to unfold. Soon we are presented with images of the ex-lover's place of business, a factory filled with obsequious, obedient employees. These employees, we're told, would follow him off a cliff like lemmings or sing in chorus, if he asked them to. Yet we are also told the ex-lover was a tour guide. By way of explanation, Rebecca describes the way this man would go to the local railway station and walk down the platform, snatching babies, screaming, from their mothers' arms.

As the images pile up in unsettling juxtaposition to one another, it becomes clear that Pinter is making oblique references to some sort of totalitarian state and some sort of mass destruction of human life. The images of sobbing mothers on a railway platform suggest the mass incarceration of Jews in World War II, for example, and the workers, we're told, are making lamps, but not ordinary lamps, which hints at the horrific objects made from human flesh in Nazi factories.

Yet the playwright never explicitly confirms any of these intimations. Nor does he attack the ex-lover, the complicit Rebecca, or the totalitarian state, which seems to have served as the backdrop for their sexual power games.

Attacking institutions as such is beyond Pinter's purpose.

It is the unsettling forces of the unconscious mind that are his concern. He seeks to summon them up, expose us to their antirational, irresistible aura, and then leave us to ponder the way in which we have been caught in an inexplicable current of menace and mystery.

There is one more major technique discovered by the surrealists in their quest for a drama that would bring this vision of mystery to the stage: They taught themselves never to take seriously the forms and conventions of life passed on to us by tradition. After all, if we are to discover new truths and new layers of meaning on the stage, no matter what our style of writing, we must begin by freeing ourselves from the grip of what has come in the past. But where other artists might rage at, or attack, the forms and conventions passed on to us by tradition, those who approach their work with the surrealist vision of life seem to rise above both anger and the hope for change that must underlie any sort of attack. Instead, the surrealist seeks to free us from the limitations of conventional perceptions by the use of good-natured ridicule.

And the more sacrilegious the act of ridicule, the better.

Alfred Jarry fired the first volley of outrageous ridicule at the norms of traditional drama. In his watershed romp, *King Ubu*, we are joyously freed from stuffy pretension in a way few other dramas have managed. On one level, the play is a devastating send-up of Shakespeare's *Macbeth*. But it goes to such extremes in its irreverent abuse of Elizabethan forms and themes that it transcends mere satire. It becomes its own, unique celebration of human willfulness and the delights of the id. The title character, Ubu, prompted by his wife to seize the throne, accomplishes this goal by using his most deadly weapon: cr-r-r-a-a-a-apping on people. Nonsense dialogue, Punch-and-Judy violence, and ridiculous battlefield encounters are crammed into the play from start to finish as Jarry willfully, playfully, joyfully tears down the most hallowed tradition of all, Shakespearean tragedy.

But it was Jean Cocteau who fused and refined all of the techniques of surrealist drama into a startling and irrefutable new vision of life. In Cocteau's full-length plays, his essential strategy was to take a timeless myth, recast it into ordinary, everyday situations, and then charge that ordinary life with new magic through the introduction of inexplicable, provocative images.

For example, in his play *Orpheus*, his basic material is drawn from the myth of the great lovers Orpheus and Eurydice. So great was their love that a jealous Hades snatched Eurydice away into the underworld. Using the unsurpassed power of his music, Orpheus lulled all the creatures guarding Eurydice to sleep and rescued her. In the original myth, the lovers meet with a tragic ending and, at the last moment, Eurydice is snatched away forever into the bowels of hell.

Cocteau takes this much-revered myth and begins by asking, What if they'd both escaped, settled down, and gotten married? In *Orpheus*, we meet the great lovers as a middle-aged, modern married couple. Orpheus the song-writer is having a creative block. Desperate for inspiration, he becomes obsessed with the ability of his pet horse to tap out words in the dirt, hoping against hope that he'll get his next great song if only he watches long enough. Eurydice, meanwhile, has become a bored housewife who breaks the living room window every week so the handsome glass repairman will come and fix it.

It is what I call playful sacrilege, and it is a direct descendant of the liberating insanity of Ubu's world. But ridiculing Greek mythology is only the starting point for Cocteau's surrealist strategy. He is not trying to write a satirical farce. He is trying to break the hold tradition has on us, so that we can rediscover the magic of the world ourselves—new, fresh, and for the first time.

And in his play, he lets us know immediately that we are dealing with a world that transcends ordinary reality.

First off, there are his very explicit stage directions. We are told we're in Greece, in Orpheus' villa, but it is a strange room, like the room a magician might live in. The sky is April blue and the light is clear, but still we feel the room is surrounded by mysterious forces. Even the most familiar objects have a suspicious air about them. Among other mysterious features, there is a white horse living inside a small "corral" in the center of the room. The horse, Cocteau advises us, has legs that look a lot like a man's. In fact, this is because an actor has to be inside the horse to accomplish the various movements it will perform. The rest of the animal is merely a facade, a cardboard cutout from the breast upward. In addition, there is a full-length mirror with a false panel through which people can enter and leave.

But most striking of all is this: apart from the blue sky, and a single strip of red on the horse's corral, there is no color in the scenery. We are told that the set must look like a cardboard cutout. And as the scene opens, the horse onstage is dictating poetry to Orpheus by tapping his hoof on the floor. Soon the horse will begin to speak, uttering oracular prophecies. And when the glazier arrives to repair the broken windowpane, Orpheus will accidentally remove the chair he's standing on, leaving the man to float, unperturbed, in midair.

Playful sacrilege. Mystery-laden images. A disturbing air of menace.

These are the hallmarks of the surrealist style.

André Breton, possibly the greatest of the surrealist thinkers, declared that the purpose of surrealism is to express the real process of human thought. And true human thought is neither logic-driven nor deliberate.

It is image-driven. And it is spontaneous.

It operates in the absence of any and all control that is exercised by reason, and it operates free of all outside considerations of aesthetics or morals.

Summary of the Surrealist Vision

In the surrealist vision of life, we seek to re-create onstage the experience of being provoked by forces that are too mysterious to yield to ordinary logic. We express the belief that the world is driven by urges and impulses that cannot be explained in rational language but which constitute the true source of human behavior.

Surrealist Action Structure

Surrealist plays are often built around an action or a series of actions undertaken by the characters; that is to say, the characters are trying to produce change in their world. However, these surface or conventional actions are primarily intended to provide the playwright with the opportunity to conjure provocative images on the stage.

1. The changes pursued by characters can be deadly serious.

2. They can be intended either to alter an increasingly menacing situation or to acquire profoundly important information.

3. The changes pursued by the characters can also be patently foolish, actions we the audience are not supposed to take seriously.

4. However, even if the playwright and the audience realize that what the characters are doing is foolish, the characters themselves take their attempts at producing change quite seriously.

5. The actions undertaken by the characters are almost always beside the point. They serve as a red herring while the playwright works a deeper and more profound strategy of marshalling his or her images onstage, images that will interact inexplicably and lead us to a new way of thinking about the events and the characters.

As you can see, although surrealist plays are often built around an attempt by the characters to produce change, change as such is of little importance to one possessed by the surrealist vision of life. Tapping into the subterranean forces of the human experience and of life itself is the true concern of the surrealist. Playwrights who labored at bringing this vision to the stage developed a range of techniques, and the most significant ones follow.

6. Images of ordinary things can be juxtaposed in unexpected and provocative ways. This will draw out or suggest deep, inarticulable significance, and the presence of unknowable forces.

7. Recognizable, everyday events, characters, or places can be stripped of their details until they take on powerful, metaphysical dimensions. At this point, they may no longer be identifiable as ordinary events, characters, or places, but may seem instead to be wholly imaginary.

8. Familiar images, objects, and situations often have lurking beneath the surface portentous or menacing qualities. Draw out these disturbing undercurrents to charge the scene with mystery.

9. Manipulate ordinary objects and images in playful ways. Turn the ordinary into the delightful or the whimsical. By doing this, you will make your audience question their normal logic and habitual expectations.

10. Any of these goals can be accomplished by manipulating actual objects or persons onstage, or through the words uttered by the characters.

Background to the Development
of Surrealism

As I mentioned at the beginning of Part Four, surrealism and expressionism first appeared at roughly the same time, the end of the nineteenth century. But for both aesthetic forms, it was World War I that provided the galvanizing catalyst, proving that both aesthetic voices were potent new ways of expressing the fears and terrors of the modern world.

When surrealism first became a recognized banner for rallying disaffected artists, it was under a different name: Dada. The name was adopted in 1915 by a group of artists in Zurich who were drawn to the sensationalistic, the shocking, and the iconoclastic in their writing, painting, and theatrical performances. *Dada* was apparently chosen at random from a German-French dictionary and refers to a child's rocking horse. The art and the antics they displayed at their headquarters, the Cabaret Voltaire, were specifically designed to outrage public audiences, who nevertheless were drawn to their performances almost as though to a circus sideshow.

By 1922, surrealism proper had begun to take form and was increasingly used as a way of accessing the irrational and unsettling side of human experience that had been so spontaneously expressed by Dada. André Breton published *The First Surrealist Manifesto* in 1924 and followed with a second one in 1929. Breton's analysis of the movement remains the most important theoretical writing on the subject, although ironically, he was steadfast in his belief that surrealism could never succeed on the stage.

In his manifesto, Breton declared that surrealism is intended to express—orally, in writing, or by other means—the real process of thought, liberated from logic or other restricting formalities. Human thought, he stated, is not a formal process at all, and it cannot be held accountable to either moral or aesthetic rules.

By its very nature surrealism is a mystifying and confusing style of art. Consequently, it took a long time before the public became familiar enough with its vocabulary to accept it readily. After Breton, the movement went into decline until 1936, when it was suddenly revived and given a permanent life in Western aesthetic by a group of painters and their sensational exhibit, called the International Surrealist Exhibition. Although initially attacked by confused and outraged art critics, the exhibition brought to the public eye names and artwork that are now routinely associated with the word *surreal*—Salvador Dali, René Magritte, and Marcel Duchamp foremost among them.

Even today, when the playwright struggling to master this vision on the stage seeks an inspiring, intuitive sense of the goals and techniques of surrealism, the paintings of Dali and Magritte contain many important clues. The inexplicable power exuded by the way these masters juxtapose provocative images is in and of itself a surreal process of thought, a surreal argument if you will, for the potency of this disturbing view of life.

13

Afternote

A Few Words from Expressionism and Surrealism

Expressionism

It is often the case that the labels created to describe new movements in art are affixed after the fact by critics and theorists, not by the artists themselves. This is certainly true of expressionism. The term first appeared in an effort to describe the work of English writers in the mid-nineteenth century who were struggling to find new ways to express themselves, but it was later adopted by German art critics who were at a loss to explain radical new experiments in nonrepresentational art going on at the end of the century. As these new experiments began to coalesce around certain techniques of distortion and abstraction, the term *expressionism* began to take on specific connotations. It came to mean art or theatre that takes objects, persons, or events from everyday life and distorts them grotesquely in order to express the nightmarish pain of the human psyche.

The term *expressionism* can sometimes be better understood when contrasted with another aesthetic form that grew up at the same time: *impressionism*.

Impressionism is a word we associate most commonly with the paintings of Monet, Degas, and Seurat, among others. In painting, it refers to the use of discontinuous, fragmented brush strokes, assembled together to give the impression of something in the real world, rather than re-creating it with the appearance of scientific accuracy in the way most classical art does.

Impressionism was later adapted to music, literature, and film, but in every case the artist is using fragments to give the impression of something we will recognize from the real world.

Expressionism, by contrast, can be thought of as a way to express or convey to others what is inside the artist, whereas impressionism conveys to others the artist's perception of the outside world.

But it is important to remember that in its most precise meaning, expressionism involves the use of grotesque distortion to achieve its goals.

Since the term became accepted, other uses of it have appeared. Between World Wars I and II, a school of expressionists appeared in the Weimar Republic. They had a specific agenda for expressionism. They believed that this radical, disturbing art form could be used to bring down governments and promote social change. This style is called German expressionism. To us today it might seem naïve to believe that art could produce social change, but both Hitler and his Communist successors in the eastern part of that country realized how dangerous the German expressionists actually were. The artists who refused to abandon expressionism were hounded out of the country or rounded up and executed.

Now the term *expressionism* is used less rigorously, and it will often appear as a convenient way to describe any art that deviates from reality in a colorful way.

Surrealism

Surrealism and *Dada* are both terms that were devised by the men and women working in those styles and were consciously applied by the artists to themselves. These terms were, if you will, rallying cries or banners under which the artists gathered.

The playwright Guillaume Apollinaire coined the word *surrealism* in the preface to his hilarious sexual-political romp *The Breasts of Tiresias.* He created the word to inform the world that he was fed up with naturalism and wanted a new style of art, one that sought out a higher realism. In an effort to explain the idea that there are more effective forms of human thought than mere rationalism, he used this example:

When man wanted to imitate walking, he created the wheel. The wheel looks nothing like feet or legs but nevertheless accomplished what its inventor(s) had in mind.

This is an example of surreal thinking, Apollinaire tells us—truth arrived at by *not* imitating reality.

André Breton, the novelist, poet, and literary critic who took up the banner of surrealism in the 1920s, expanded considerably on Apollinaire's thoughts, drawing heavily from the work of Freud. Breton often used dreams and the irrational language of dreams as an analogy for the surreal experience. As a result, the words *surreal* and *dreamlike* have become interchangeable in common usage. But there are more complex and sublime notions at work when the word *surreal* is applied to art of any kind and theatre in particular.

There are some useful guidelines that can help the writer/artist distinguish between expressionism and surrealism:

- Surrealism is not grotesquely distorted. If distorted at all, it may verge on the grotesque, but it never quite achieves the repellent and corrosive commentary of expressionism.

- Surrealism is not a medium of articulable ideas. In an expressionist work, the theme of the writer or painter can usually be summarized because it is based on an idea that can be articulated, often in a single sentence. But in fully developed surrealism, this is seldom the case.

14

A Closer Look at Three Powerful Voices

Important playwrights have been using the ideas that form the core of this book over the last hundred and fifty years to create unforgettable theatre experiences and to communicate in unique ways their own personal visions of life. Plays like *The Glass Menagerie, Waiting for Godot,* and *Death of a Salesman* have dazzled and thrilled us since their earliest performances specifically because of the way in which each author subtly intermingled a range of writing techniques to create a unique and breathtaking work of art.

When Tennessee Williams fused the structure of realism with the psychology of naturalism in *The Glass Menagerie* and *A Streetcar Named Desire* and then electrified his characters with the ethos of romanticism, it was the equivalent of Rembrandt using forced perspective, dry brushing, and modeling techniques to create an unforgettable canvas. Yet, to a large extent, the theatre community is not comfortable discussing plays the same way that painters discuss techniques of the brush. If there is anything radical in this book, it would be the desire to correct that shortcoming and to empower today's playwrights with the language, structural insights, and underlying ideas that have driven great theatre for all of the modern period.

I have tended to focus in each chapter on works that were relatively straightforward examples of each style being discussed. So it seems right to take some time now to show the way in which great playwrights have taken a little bit from each of these playwriting models in order to create a unique voice, designed to express exactly what each individual author has learned about life, what each individual author needs to share with an audience. If you will, the basic playwriting models of the last 150 years have served as bolts of cloth from which each playwright has tailored a garment cut perfectly to embody the vision that drove him or her to write.

In 1994, the great American theatrical pioneer and playwright Edward Albee unveiled in New York his latest work, *Three Tall Women*. A critical and commercial success, the play was one of only a few successful straight dramas produced in New York in recent years. Not being a musical or a play with spectacular settings and stage effects, it gives us an important reason to sit up and pay attention. With the simplest of scenery and a cast that, almost in its entirety, consisted of just three actresses, Albee created an event that challenged and satisfied audiences, firing the theatre world with excitement.

How did he accomplish this? What truths did Albee tap into with this play in order to reach his audience so effectively?

When one sits in the theatre and watches *Three Tall Women*, the play seems hardly surprising, almost a bit like watching a television drama, in fact. The setting is the perfectly ordinary bedroom of an elderly, wealthy woman who is dying. A middle-aged woman of fifty-two and a younger woman of twenty-six attend on her. We're not quite sure what their exact relationship to the dying woman is, however. At first it seems they might be estranged daughters, but after a while it becomes clear that they are receiving money for their services. The fifty-two-year-old appears to be a home companion or a nurse. The twenty-six-year-old works for the law firm that handles some of the old woman's personal affairs. Yet they speak easily and somewhat intimately with one another, as though they were family, making the kind of barbed or veiled commentary typical of estranged family members.

The dialogue also has a vaguely circular construction to it. The old woman makes ongoing references to a "he" whose identity is never clearly established. It's someone she's waiting for, and even though she yearns for him to show up, she doesn't believe he will. She repeats, almost senselessly, allegations that she's being robbed by people around her. And like the Old Man in Ionesco's *The Chairs*, she returns intermittently to a rambling story about her earlier life, a story that seems to go nowhere.

The use of the most fundamental devices from the theatre of the absurd in Act I is not a coincidence. Few authors in America know absurdism as well as Albee, who helped introduce it here to begin with. Yet the scene is not absurdist in the extreme way a Beckett or an Ionesco play is. On the surface it has all the appearances of realism. It is stripped down to its bare essentials, driven by causally constructed exchanges between the characters. Even the old woman's ramblings are driven by causality, since they stem from old age and advancing senility. In fact, at first blush, *Three Tall Women* might be mistaken for a realist play examining the issues of old age and death, as though these are problems that can be solved.

Although the absurdism in the play never takes center stage, announcing that we are in an alternate reality the way it would in a play by Beckett or Ionesco, nevertheless it serves an indispensable function.

For in Act II, we do indeed enter an alternate reality. It is a transition we have been unconsciously primed to make by the very absurdist touches, hidden beneath the surfaces, I have just mentioned.

The curtain before intermission falls just as the old woman, having revealed a particularly poignant and heart-breaking event that occurred with her late husband when they were young, suffers a minor stroke. The home companion advises us she is not dead, and she will be fine.

Curtain up on Act II.

The elderly woman is lying in bed as before, only now she wears an oxygen mask. We are told in the stage directions that the two younger women attending on her are wearing different clothes. This is no small detail, for in moments we are to learn that none of the characters is who she seems.

The first four lines of dialogue accomplish in microcosm what Albee's strategy has been so far for the entire play: They trick us into thinking this is a normal, realist situation when it is not now and never has been.

The home companion character, gazing at the immobile figure of the old woman, announces that there has been no change. We assume she means no change in the old woman's medical condition, that is, she is still alive, as she was at the end of Act I.

The lawyer's assistant is wistful and reluctant to accept this proclamation. We assume she wishes the old woman to get better.

The home companion then replies sharply that that's the way it goes, this condition never changes, you can be certain it will happen to both of us. When the younger woman protests that she doesn't want to think about it, the middle-aged woman suggests that, yes, she should think about it, even as young as she is.

We realize they are not talking about the old woman's condition at all.

They are talking about death. And they are offering insights into death that seem eerily well-informed, almost preternatural.

This helps prepare us for our next shock.

For within moments, the old woman herself enters, even as an exact replica of her lies dying in the bed before them.

The old woman is dressed in a beautiful lavender dress, and this completes the visual transition in the habiliment of the three women, helping us recognize that they are, all three of them, different versions of the dying woman—versions of her that existed when she was twenty-six, fifty-two, and ninety-one years old. All three of them are, together, the character who has been at the center of the play since it started.

To see them standing there, discussing and arguing about "their" life while the body that contained them lies giving up its mortality under an oxygen mask is a potent and unnerving image.

In the subtlest possible way, Albee has utilized surrealism to achieve the effect he wants. It is not as blatant as Cocteau's talking horse or Maeterlinck's twelve blind men and women sitting with their dead priest—although it does harbor hints of the latter—but it is the final brush stroke that completes Albee's canvas. No doubt he knew, from the moment he began typing the first lines of dialogue, that he was aiming for this moment. He also knew that the cumulative effect would be surreal and disturbing, that it would shock us out of our normal ways of thinking about death, and that it would prepare us to listen to the insights he himself has gleaned over the years.

In the end, we discover that the play *is* about old age and dying.

But Albee did not want to write a comforting, realist play about reconciliation and healing. As I said before, old age and dying are not problems that can be solved. Rather, they are devastating enigmas that can only be grasped as ineffable mysteries, full of bleak yet ultimately tranquil poetry. He knew that he had to capture a vision onstage that was charged with poetic mystery. And he turned to the subtlest possible surrealist techniques to accomplish this.

A very different play that captures a poetic rendering of life's central dilemmas is Ntozake Shange's *For Colored Girls Who Have Considered Suicide When the Rainbow Is Enuf.* To some extent, Shange anticipates Albee's strategy of studying the inner heart of a woman by breaking her up into different characters onstage. A chorus of seven women represents the central character of Shange's play, each dressed in a different-colored gown. Early in the opening prologue, the chorus members announce in turn that they are standing outside of major American cities—Chicago, Detroit, Houston, and so on—and in this way alert us to their true identity: they are Everywoman, and they exist outside the mainstream of American life.

What follows in this self-proclaimed choreopoem is an evening of searing, funny, poignant, and horrific vignettes, captured in verse, recited in groups and singly by the seven chorus members. The material of each poetic "scene" is either an autobiographical recollection from the author's life—a life as disturbing and dramatic as that of any woman of color living in America—or a reflection on issues and experiences central to the lives of all women in this country. Dance and song are interspersed among the poems. The play is performed like a flow of consciousness or a quasi-improvised, spontaneous outburst of poetic musing. Yet, in spite of its apparent free-form structure, we never become impatient or bored, waiting for something to happen. This is because Shange has assembled her poems on a graceful, natural structure that, like a living skeleton, invisibly gives support and power to the proceedings.

After announcing their collective identity to us, essentially, as "she who lives outside the American mainstream," the chorus members break into a brief session of childhood games. Then they move quickly to an account of graduating high school and first sexual experiences.

Already, Shange's structure has begun to work its spell on us.

These are not randomly assembled scenes, flowing with unpremeditated spontaneity, any more than the lines memorized by actors and uttered in a fresh and startling way are spontaneous.

We are witnessing significant life passages, arranged in chronological order.

We are seeing the life of a woman of color in America, played out step-by-step before us.

At no point is the age of the central character announced, nor are any dates, nor are any chronological designations. Nevertheless, these episodes taken from the collective experience of minority women clearly play out in an order that approximates personal growth from an early age to an adult time in life. Childhood, high school, and sexual initiation are followed by two poems recounting experiences of immature love. The first describes an infatuation with the Puerto Rican musician Willie Colon, the second, a recital of all the things an adolescent woman does to get the attention of the young man who won't respond to her.

These are followed by poems describing rape and abortion.

Slowly, with exquisite imagery and painful remembrance, we are being taken through the significant experiences that are shared almost universally by women. Even rape and abortion fall under the heading "universal," because women who have escaped them invariably have close friends who have not.

Going through the play poem by poem, the verses seem to group themselves into related scenes. One way those scenes can be understood is that they flow progressively through fourteen life experiences. Certainly, other ways of grouping the poems are also possible, but fourteen is a provocative number, and once it appears it's hard to ignore. It hints at least indirectly at a parallel to the fourteen Stations of the Cross, for example. The stations in this case are secular, not religious, and the play, like Christ's journey up Calvary, does indeed chronicle a passage through life to death, finally arriving in the last, uplifting choral piece at an undeniable rebirth. More than anything else, this suggests the organizational strategies used by the expressionists. Playwrights like Ernst Toller and Georg Kaiser used this sort of progression through a series of "stations," or significant scenes, to give power to what would otherwise be a free-form collection of rambling vignettes.

And this isn't the only place from which Shange has borrowed her organizational strategies. The core idea of structuring a play around the advancing experiences of a central character was used by Brecht in both *Baal* and *Mother Courage*. It can also be found in the work of naturalist playwrights such as Chekov or Gorky, who use the advancing age of their characters from scene to scene as a key connective technique to hold our interest in their stories.

But let's go back to these fourteen episodes.

Has Shange designated them as such in her script? No, of course not. The point is that Shange knew her play needed a flowing, natural structure. So she created one by borrowing from the expressionists and the naturalists. In fact, the central conceit of telling a universal woman's story through an abstracted chorus is also expressionist.

But the expressionist influences end there. The author saw no reason to use grotesque distortion, for example, or shocking violence, or outrageous scenic effects in order to capture her own particular vision onstage. She felt free to take what she needed and to use it the way she needed.

And she fused these techniques with yet another device, one taken from epic drama.

As the play moves from one vignette to the next, it clearly jumps the span of many years. The vignettes occur in widely disparate locations around America. And although the many characters can be abstracted by the viewer into a universal woman, they also exist independently as separate people, none of which could have had all these experiences. And there are literally dozens of them.

But most remarkable of all, perhaps, is the poet/playwright's ultimate goal in the play: to tell us that change is possible.

The change that occurs is an inner one, and the universal woman who has been conjured up by the play reveals what it is, in the final choral piece, performed by all seven girls.

Here, Shange shares with us what may very well have been her own personal catharsis: how, after a night (or is it a lifetime?) of distracted inner agony, she found solace in the arms of a tree. She knew she needed healing—"a laying on of hands"—and she found it first in the sky, then deep within herself, when she recognized her own irrefutable connection to the sacred.

As she says near the end of the play, she found God in herself.

There can be no question that *For Colored Girls* is, at its heart, a journey—a journey through innocence and learning, to pain and despair, to redemption and wisdom. Throughout this journey, Shange is informed, above all, by a vision that change is possible. And even though this is ultimately a realist notion, she has convinced us her vision is true with almost no realist writing strategies at all.

Epic poetry. Expressionist technique. Naturalist structure. Realist message.

It is as if, for the most inspired playwrights, these techniques exist like separate colors on an artist's palette, to be blended and intermingled as the vision of the playwright and the needs of the canvas require.

Shange and Albee have captured, respectively, visions of change and mystery. The final example here is one that explores the vision of futility. Few plays of the last century have captured that vision in a more skillful manner than Sam Shepard's *True West*.

The play opens on a setting that is a fusion of interior and exterior realities. Half–height walls and windows reveal, outside the house, bushes, shrubbery, and sky. In addition to this, the floor is partially carpeted in artificial grass. But these vaguely surreal touches are more than offset by the unremarkable realism of the kitchen and dining nook depicted within.

Two brothers, Austin and Lee, are engaged in what at first is a low-level conflict. Austin, a screenwriter, has come here to their mother's suburban Southern California home to get some work done while she's away in Alaska. Lee has arrived unexpectedly and is trying to engage Austin in a conversation that prevents him from writing. The conversation touches on their absent mother, their indigent father, and the fact that Lee intends to spend the weekend stealing appliances from the neighbors. So far so good. Through the prism of a traditionally constructed, realist conflict, we are learning who the characters are. Furthermore, we have glimpsed some of the underlying sociological influences—that is, the mother and the father—that drive them.

These background factors continue to be hinted at as Shepard assembles the elements of his plot: Lee embarks on his mission of burglary in spite of Austin's objections, and a movie producer, Saul, arrives to discuss Austin's new project. Lee insinuates himself into the producer's good graces and pitches his own movie idea. The basic situation finally gels when Saul actually expresses interest in Lee's concept.

At first Austin is congratulatory. He humors Lee and sets out to draft a treatment of Lee's idea. But when Saul gets increasingly serious about this movie and severs his relationship with Austin, Lee finds himself on his own. Austin refuses to help write the screenplay, and we the audience discover that Shepard has pulled a neat twist on us: the opening situation is being repeated, but the roles of the characters have been reversed. For now, it's Lee who's trying to write and Austin who pointedly interrupts him over and over.

It is a device that hearkens back to the absurdist constructs of Samuel Beckett.

John Fletcher, in his seminal essays on Beckett's work, notes that *Waiting for Godot* is built around a series of repeated moments or tropes. The net effect of these repetitions is that they do away with the need for forward movement in the plot, not by the act of repeating, but by the act of repeating *imperfectly*. Fletcher calls this asymmetrical repetition. Thus, though Vladimir and Estragon consider hanging themselves in Act I, they actually experiment with it in Act II. When Estragon sleeps in Act One, he sleeps badly in Act Two. When Pozzo and Lucky return, they are physically different from when we last saw them. We, the audience, recognize the act of repetition. But it is the fact that something has been altered that tickles our intellects, provokes us into a search for hidden meanings, and makes us feel as though the play is moving toward a moment of enlightenment or revelation.

In *True West*, when we discover that Lee has become the frustrated writer and Austin the provocateur, we have unconsciously been prepared for Shepard's larger objective. He intends to take us in a complete circle. Although the stakes will go up and veiled threats will become literal ones, the essential condition of these two American brothers will not change one iota.

Even when one has killed the other.

The circular construction intensifies. We learn that, since Lee is attempting to be a writer, Austin feels he must undertake to become a burglar. Soon the kitchen has been filled with toasters that Austin spent the night stealing from neighbors. In the production directed by Gary Sinise at Steppenwolf Theatre in Chicago, Sinise himself played Austin, and he exploited the presence of the toasters onstage with a kind of ingenuity that is absolutely consistent with the absurdist vision saturating the play. He led one toaster around by the cord as though it were a pet dog, making it jump over obstacles. He stacked the toasters and bowed down before them as though they were a pagan idol. These are the sorts of circular activities that are reminiscent of Estragon and Vladimir, when they play with their hats or pretend to be Pozzo and Lucky. It is the vaudevillian shtick that Beckett has elevated for all time into our serious dramatic vocabulary. Its purpose is to keep us amused, if you will, while we wait to discover that life is pointless and nothing is going to change.

And yet things do change.

True to the vision of the absurd that has become an equal partner now with realism in this play, things get worse, because gradually the boys are destroying their mother's home. One of the most dramatic and hilarious real-izations of this process comes when Lee attempts to obtain the phone number of a woman in Bakersfield from directory assistance. His desperate search for a pencil leads him to ransack the entire kitchen, emptying shelves and cupboards onto the floor and ultimately ripping the phone off the wall.

At the end of the rampage, nothing substantive in their situation has changed, but conditions are definitely worse.

Even at this advanced point in the play, Shepard has not abandoned his initial urge to capture a world defined as much by psychology and sociology as by circularity. In the final scene, Austin and Lee's mother returns home unexpectedly. They cower before her like teenagers, sheepish and apologetic. Yet from her treatment of them, it's clear that she is the source of their dysfunctional behavior. In the culminating moments, Austin strangles Lee to death with a phone cord—only to have Lee spring to his feet to continue their never-ending struggle.

As the lights fade and they face off, their darkening silhouettes become more and more like the coyotes we have heard howling in the Southern California hills throughout the play. If anything, Shepard's point is that the rivalry between brothers—the fire in the blood that rips families apart—will continue forever.

Realism fused with absurdism. Assisted at first by a hint of the surreal, but galvanized in the end with a final, undiluted, surrealist tableau.

The lingering mystery of the play, with its enigmatic and ultimately irreducible effect on our imaginations, achieves, in fact, a surrealist stature that far exceeds the limited touches of surrealism employed within it. Above all else, we feel as though we have visited suburban America in a parallel dimension where the underlying futility of our efforts to produce change is exposed as a brutal joke. All attempts to communicate become ridiculous. All attempts to use physical force, nightmarish. All hope, fraudulent.

Mystery. Change. Futility.

There are, without question, other subtle and complex visions that form themselves in the human imagination as we seek to make sense of the world. And like colors on a painter's palette, these techniques for realizing your vision can be mixed and combined until they express what you need to share with an audience—the truths about life that you have come to recognize.

It's also important to remember that at some point, as we blend and intermingle different visions of life, our own particular way of seeing the world is elevated to a unique status that defies labels of any kind. In this way, the view of the cosmos that overtakes our writing can defy even our own ability to make sense of it or to analyze it. When that happens, our vision of life becomes an intuitively experienced, spontaneously realized approach to playwriting that comes as naturally as breathing.

But only much reflection, and a great deal of writing, will bring the playwright to that point—the point at which what you have learned and need to share form the fabric and the cut of everything you write.

"Why do I write?"

There are a hundred answers to that question, but foremost among them is the need to share what we have learned, to communicate what we have experienced.

Can you understand the importance of the events I have lived through? Can you see the world that I see? Can you hear me?